Resource Pack 3

Group work skills

Written by
Dr Val Harris

Contents

■ **Day 5** Session 9 and 10

Session plan 9 and 10

Session 9

Session 10

■ **Day 6** Session 11 and 12

Session plan 11 and 12

Session 11

Session 12

Note

To aid your use of this material, pages intended as Tutor Prompt Sheets, Worksheets, Handouts, Case Studies or Reflective Journals have been given an appropriate mark in the top right-hand corners, as shown below.

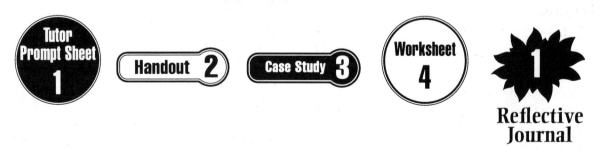

Introduction

This resource pack has been produced by the Federation for Community Development Learning as part of its ongoing commitment to develop and share community development learning practice. The pack is part of a series which is linked to the Open College Network Community Development Programme (see www.fcdl.org.uk or www.syocn.org.uk).

The Programme was developed out of an initial set of courses run by Salford Council for Voluntary Service as part of its community work training programme. The courses were rewritten by Salford CVS and Dr. Val Harris in order to map them to the revised National Occupational Standards for Community Development Work (see www.fcdl.org.uk or www.paulo.org.uk). The Salford units became the first training courses to be mapped to the revised standards in 2002.

The Federation, working with the co-operation of Salford CVS, has accredited the programme through South Yorkshire Open College Network. It has been designed so that further units may be included as and when appropriate. A subsequent set of units has been added to the original list and will be accredited through the OCN Community Development Programme.

The Federation has worked with the Open College Network to develop a National Community Development Award based on this programme. This is the first national community development award that uses the OCN process. It adds to the growing number of qualifications and progression routes for community development workers, managers and activists. For further information on the national award, please contact the Federation or NOCN (www.nocn.org.uk).

A full programme

This resource pack relates to one of the units in the OCN Community Development Programme and can be used to form part of the national award. The programme covers training courses and materials for a range of qualifications levels. To date, these include foundation (1), intermediate (2) and advanced (3) levels. For further information, see the Get Accredited publication produced by the Federation and OCN.

The programme has been endorsed by the England Standards Board for Community Development Work Training and Qualifications. Additional units will continue to be developed and added to the programme.

The full set of units (to be accompanied by resource packs) is listed on the next page.

Level 1

1. Understanding community development work
2. Community development work skills
3. Reflective practice.

Level 2

1. Understanding community development work
2. Community development work skills
3. Effective partnership working
4. Monitoring and evaluation
5. Funding and resources
6. Publicity skills
7. Involving people in community development
8. Planning for community groups
9. Group work skills
10. Developing community organisations
11. Reflective practice
12. Social Justice
13. Identifying needs

14. Neighbourhood regeneration
15. Representing a community of interest/identity
16. Principles into practice.

Level 3

1. Effective partnership working
2. Monitoring and evaluation
3. Funding and resources
4. Publicity skills
5. Involving people in community development
6. Planning for community groups
7. Group work skills
8. Developing community organisations
9. Reflective practice
10. Social Justice
11. Identifying needs
12. Neighbourhood regeneration
13. Representing a community of interest/identity
14. Principles into practice.

Using the resource pack

The packs are written in six blocks of 2-hour sessions so that training sessions can be organised flexibly to meet the needs of participants. They are designed to be run with crêches, in evenings, to fit school times etc., and the 2-hour blocks can be added together.

For each four hours of learning there is one learning outcome so that these blocks can be run as stand alone sessions and people can slowly build up their portfolios if they want to. There are learning journal questions, worksheets, etc., to enable participants to gather evidence of their learning from each session.

Each 2-hour session contains:

◆ A detailed session plan
◆ Tutor prompt sheets
◆ Handouts
◆ Exercises, including case studies, work sheets, role plays, stories and games to support each session.

The pack includes everything you need to run the sessions, however, the materials can be adapted and changed to meet both the trainer's style and the needs of participants. The case studies and other exercises might not be relevant to the participants but do give an example which can be adapted by the trainer.

Developing new resources

The Federation welcomes any feedback and ideas for exercises for the next reprint. This resource pack forms part of a series of publications around community development learning produced by the Federation. For further information, please contact the Federation on 0114 273 9391 or info@fcdl.org.uk

Unit title(s): **Group Work Skills**

Credit value: One   **Level:** Two

Learning Outcome The learner will be able to:	Assessment criteria **The learner has achieved the outcome because s/he can:**	Evidence Number	Assessor	Moderator
1. Understand the reasons why people become involved in community groups/networks	1.1 Describe the range of motivations and expectations that people may have when joining a community group/network			
2. Understand group dynamics and the potential for conflict to arise	2.1 Describe the basics of group dynamics with reference to a particular group 2.2 Suggest ways of defusing or handling potential conflicts			
3. Understand the processes involved when a group/network sets its objectives and priorities	3.1 Describe two participatory techniques for involving group/network members in setting its aims and objectives 3.2 Identify two issues of communication that can arise in groups/networks and suggest ways to improve communication			

Evidence matrix

v

Evidence matrix

4. Appreciate the different ways or organising collectively and understand what makes an effective group/network	4.1 Identify the range of roles that need to be taken in a group/network 4.2 Explain how people's skills and experience can be used effectively within a group/network 4.3 Suggest two ways to support and encourage active participation by group/network members	
5. Understand the issues of inclusion and exclusion within groups/networks	5.1 Identify some of the processes which can lead to groups/networks becoming exclusive 5.2 Suggest two ways that a group/network can remain open and inclusive	
6. Demonstrate an awareness of the roles they take in groups and the impact they have on a group	6.1 Explain the key roles they take in groups 6.2 Describe the key interpersonal skills needed to work effectively within a group	

Unit title(s): **Group Work Skills**

Credit value: One   **Level:** Three

Learning Outcome	Assessment criteria	Evidence Number	Assessor	Moderator
The learner will be able to:	**The learner has achieved the outcome because s/he can:**			
1. Understand the reasons why people become involved in community groups/networks	1.1 Analyse the reasons for people joining a group and the implications this can have for a group/network			
2. Understand group dynamics and the potential for conflict to arise	2.1 Reflect on the relevance of the life cycle of groups in relation to a particular group 2.2 Analyse the likely cause of tensions within community groups/networks and suggest ways to deal with any resulting conflicts			
3. Understand the processes involved when a group/network sets its objectives and priorities	3.1 Analyse the merits of the different methods available to groups/networks to establish their aims and objectives 3.2 Explain their role in assisting a group/network to agree its purpose and structure 3.3 Identify communication blocks that need to be negotiated and resolved			

Evidence matrix

vii

Evidence matrix

	4.1	Analyse the different roles taken within a group/network and explain why they are important			
4. Appreciate the different ways or organising collectively and understand what makes an effective group/network	4.1	Analyse the different roles taken within a group/network and explain why they are important			
	4.2	Describe, with examples, different ways that groups/networks can organise to meet their aims and objectives			
5. Understand the issues of inclusion and exclusion within groups/ networks	5.1	Analyse the issues around inclusion and exclusion that relate to groups/networks			
	5.2	Describe how they could devise a strategy to ensure that a group remains inclusive and open			
6. Demonstrate an awareness of the roles they take in groups and the impact they have on a group	6.1	Describe their role within groups and analyse the factors that affect these roles			
	6.2	Describe the key interpersonal skills required for effective group work over a period of time and suggest how these can be developed within a group			

Group Work Skills • **Evidence Matrix**
Federation for Community Development Learning

Introduction to the key issues

Introduction to the key issues
Session Plan 1 and 2

◆ **Target audience**

People involved in and working with community groups

◆ **Length of session**

2 x 2-hour sessions; four hours in total

◆ **Session aim(s)**

● To provide an introduction to some of the key issues relating to group work within a community setting

◆ **Session outcomes**

At the end of the session students/trainees will...

● Demonstrate an understanding of the reasons why people become involved in community groups/networks

◆ **Indicative content**

● Value of collective working

● Issues in community groups

● Life cycle of groups

● Understanding community groups

● Potential and problems in community groups

● Why people join groups – different expectations and motivations.

Detailed Session Plan 1

Time	Content	Exercise/Method	Resources	Notes *core topic or optional if time*
0.00	Welcome and domestics	Tutor input	Tutor info sheet	Adapt list to venue
0.05	Introductory game	Name game	Tutor Prompt Sheet 1	
0.20	Aims of the course and OCN accreditation	Tutor input	Tutor Prompt Sheet 2 Handout 1 OCN forms	
0.30	Ground rules	Small groups to discuss what they would like to see; put onto post-it notes and tutor to collate and get agreement. Tutor to link to need for all groups to have ground rules	Tutor Prompt Sheet 3 Post-it notes Flip chart and pens	
0.55	Hope and fears	In pairs; introduce themselves to each other and make lists; feedback to whole group and tutor to respond	Tutor Prompt Sheet 4	

Group Work Skills • **Session One**
Federation for Community Development Learning

Detailed Session Plan 1

Time	Content	Exercise/Method	Resources	Notes
				core topic or optional if time
1.20	Key purpose – emphasis on the collective action and practice principle of working and learning together	Tutor input on key purpose and importance of collective action	Tutor Prompt Sheet 5 Handout 2	
1.30	Value of collective action – what it can achieve	Three small groups to look at two of the values statements and associated practice principles. Ask them to consider where collective action might be involved – giving examples	Tutor Prompt Sheet 5 Handout 3	
1.55	Collective action and the individual	Tutor input on linking individual struggles/concerns into collective action	Tutor Prompt Sheet 5	
2.00	End			

Domestic checklist

◆ Tell people about:

    1. Fire exits and procedures; and if people leave early they should let tutors know so that the register can be amended

    2. Toilets

    3. Break times and where refreshments are served

    4. Smoking areas

◆ Give out any forms

◆ Remember to make a notice for the door.

The first warm up exercise

As this is the beginning of a group work course it would be appropriate to either give everyone name badges or pens and labels to make their own.

Explain to people that as it is the first time they have all met, you would like them to think that they are at a conference or networking event where people are milling around.

Then ask people to begin to move around the room and greet everyone present and introduce themselves and their group/organisation. They can greet people in whatever way feels appropriate, such as bowing, shaking hands, smiling.

You may need to remind people to think about the appropriateness of touching other people who they have just met, or indeed even those they know well.

Aims of the course

You can either flip the aims of the course or use Handout 1 to give to people. You should talk through the key areas that the course will cover and be prepared to clarify any points that people want to raise. Explain that these are key headings and there will be an opportunity in the first two sessions for participants to add in other issues they would like the course to cover and you will see what is possible to organise.

You need to explain that this course can lead to OCN accreditation at levels 2/3 and that this means:

◆ That to some extent the syllabus is set so that people can meet the criteria for the award, so it may not be possible to deviate too much from the main topics

◆ That people can choose what level they can present their work at; Level 2 expects people to be able to describe issues and problems and to suggest how they could be tackled. Level 3 asks for an analysis of situations and their roles within this aspect of community development work. If people are not clear about the levels it may help if you explain it as the difference between GCSEs and A levels.

◆ Reflective journal questions will be available at both levels, and people need to complete them after each four hours of group work and learning. You will give feedback on their work and maybe help them decide what level is appropriate.

The aims of the course

To provide an insight into the workings of community based groups and how to make them more effective. The key areas to be covered include:

◆ Understanding why people get involved in community groups

◆ Understanding the dynamics that can develop in groups

◆ Exploring conflicts within groups

◆ How groups decide on their aims and objectives

◆ Communication within groups

◆ Different ways to organise within groups

◆ Developing and sustaining inclusive groups

◆ The roles that people take and how that affects groups.

The aims of the course

This course aims to provide an insight into the workings of community based groups and how to make them more effective.

The **key areas** to be covered include:

◆ Understanding why people get involved in community groups

◆ Understanding the dynamics that can develop in groups

◆ Exploring conflicts within groups

◆ How groups decide on their aims and objectives

◆ Communication within groups

◆ Different ways to organise within groups

◆ Developing and sustaining inclusive groups

◆ The roles that people take and how that affects a group.

Ground rules

Split the group into four smaller groups and ask them to think about what ground rules they would want for this course in order for them to get the most from the learning and to enable them to contribute to the course.

Give each group a number of post-it notes and ask them to write one thing on each.

When the buzz has died down call the group back together; ask for one post-it note and then ask for any more on the same lines. Place all the similar ones together on a flip chart. Clarify what is meant by each of them and get some group agreement on what is acceptable, especially around:

◆ Confidentiality – is it personal and organisational information that stays in the room?

◆ Anti-oppressive behaviour – what do we mean and who should be challenging and how?

◆ General statements like 'respecting others opinions' need to be discussed in relation to the other rules – do we have to listen to people's views we find offensive and against the values of community development work?

Once you have taken all their points, say that you will summarise them at the next break and come back with a list for them to agree upon, but that for now you would expect them to abide by the rules they have agreed.

You should conclude by making the link between this exercise here and the need for all groups to have their own ground rules so that people know how they work, and there are less mixed or unsaid messages flying around which often leads to conflicts within groups.

You may want to develop your own check list of what you want in the ground rules to protect yourself and make sure that they are included in the final list.

Some examples maybe:

◆ We will keep to the start and finish times and the times set by the trainer

◆ All mobile phones to be switched off during the session (emergency telephone number for the centre is xxxxxxxxxx)

◆ We will respect each other and our different views. We will take care not to offend others by our language and/or behaviour

◆ We will listen carefully to each other and allow people to finish. We will try not to hog the conversation

◆ We will keep personal and organisational information confidential to the group

◆ We can ask for clarification about comments/ instructions if necessary.

Hopes and fears

This is the first opportunity for people to express their interest and concerns about the course and for you to gauge the interests and the level of the course members.

Put people into pairs – at this stage it doesn't matter if people know their partner as some people may feel more confident to stay with those they came with or know. Ask them to make two lists; one of their hopes for this course and the second of any concerns they may have.

In the feedback session ask the first pair to give one example of a hope, write this on the flip and check if any other groups have the same. Ask the next pair for a different hope, and repeat the process until all the hopes are written on the flip chart. Summarise where you think that you will be able to cover their ideas – for example, using a range of methods, making it relevant to their community development work, etc. Then repeat with their fears/concerns.

You may want to answer some of their fears/concerns as they arise, for example:

◆ You may not want to do role play but there may be times when its helpful to practice our skills in, for example, getting our point across in a meeting. However, there will be opportunities for observer roles and we won't be putting people on the spot.

There may be some non-negotiable points:

◆ If you are going to miss more than 20% of the programme you will not be able to submit for the award – sorry! But it did say that on the publicity

◆ If you may need to be contacted urgently because of your home circumstances, then give those people the phone number of the venue and a message will be passed through to you. Leaving your phone on will disrupt the group, and you may be dealing with other phone calls and not just the one you are waiting for.

And then there will be some where you can agree to accommodate concerns.

Key Purpose, Values and Practice Principles

Give out the key purpose statement (Handout 2) and read it out. Emphasise the collective nature of community development work and how this makes it different from other occupations such as social work which are more individual and family focused.

Give out Handout 3 and explain how community development has always had a clear values base and this is our best attempt to make these explicit. Explain that there are six key value statements and in the National Occupational Standards for Community Development Work there are explanations of what these values might mean in our practice. These are called practice principles – they are not exclusive but aim to give some idea of how we can put the values into practice.

Organise three smaller groups and give each group two of the values and practice principles to look at. Ask them to look at where collective action might be relevant, and if they can to think of some examples.

Take the feedback from each group, asking other groups to add in any comments or other examples. You should expect there to be some overlap between the discussions as inevitable the values tend to intertwine with each other.

Summarise this session by talking about the link of individual struggles and collective action. It is often the situation that someone finds themselves in that gives the impetus for a more collective approach, as they realise that they can't do it on their own. Community development doesn't deny the importance of individuals and their situation. It just works on the basis that working collectively is more effective and that by working in groups people will develop their skills and knowledge which they can use in other parts of their lives.

The key purpose of community development work

The key purpose of community development work is collectively to bring about social change and justice, by working with communities[1] to:

◆ identify their needs, opportunities, rights and responsibilities

◆ plan, organise and take action

◆ evaluate the effectiveness and impact of the action

all in ways which challenge oppressions and tackle inequalities.

1. *'Communities' refer to those which can be defined geographically or those defined by interest or identity.*

The values of community development work

◆ **Social Justice**

Working towards a fairer society that respects civil and human rights and challenges oppression

◆ **Self-determination**

Individuals and groups have the right to identify shared issues and concerns as the starting point for collective action

◆ **Working and Learning together**

Valuing and using the skills, knowledge, experience and diversity within communities to collectively bring about desired changes

◆ **Sustainable Communities**

Empowering communities to develop their independence and autonomy whilst making and maintaining links to the wider society

◆ **Participation**

Everyone has the right to fully participate in the decision-making processes that affect their lives

◆ **Reflective Practice**

Effective community development is informed and enhanced through reflection on action.

Practice principles

Social Justice

◆ Respecting and valuing diversity and difference

◆ Challenging oppressive and discriminatory actions and attitudes

◆ Addressing power imbalances between individuals, within groups and society

◆ Committing to pursue civil and human rights for all

◆ Seeking and promoting policy and practices that are just and enhance equality whilst challenging those that are not.

Sustainable Communities

◆ Promoting the empowerment of individuals and communities

◆ Supporting communities to develop their skills to take action

◆ Promoting the development of autonomous and accountable structures

◆ Learning from experiences as a basis for change

◆ Promoting effective collective and collaborative working

◆ Using resources with respect for the environment.

Self-determination

◆ Valuing the concerns or issues that communities identify as their starting points

◆ Raising people's awareness of the range of choices open to them, providing opportunities for discussion of implications of options

◆ Promoting the view that communities do not have the right to oppress other communities

◆ Working with conflict within communities.

Participation

◆ Promoting the participation of individuals and communities, particularly those traditionally marginalised/excluded

◆ Recognising and challenging barriers to full and effective participation

◆ Supporting communities to gain skills to engage in participation

◆ Developing structures that enable communities to participate effectively

◆ Sharing good practice in order to learn from each other.

Working and Learning Together

◆ Demonstrating that collective working is effective

◆ Supporting and developing individuals to contribute effectively to communities

◆ Developing a culture of informed and accountable decision making

◆ Ensuring all perspectives within the community are considered

◆ Sharing good practice in order to learn from each other.

Reflective Practice

◆ Promoting and supporting individual and collective learning through reflection on practice

◆ Changing practice in response to outcomes of reflection

◆ Recognising the constraints and contexts within which community development takes place

◆ Recognising the importance of keeping others informed and updated about the wider context.

Detailed Session Plan 2

Time	Content	Exercise/Method	Resources	Notes *core topic or optional if time*
0.00	Wake up	Any gentle moving game if after lunch		
0.10	(Recap on) life cycle of groups	Buzz groups for people to discuss what they know about the ups and downs of groups lives. Tutor summary. Whole group discussion on what this might mean for working with groups	Tutor Prompt Sheet 6 Handout 4 on life cycle of groups from other course and different models	
0.45	What range of groups are people involved in?	Each person is given post-it notes and asked to write down the name and type of group(s) they are involved in. Pin up large continuum of different kinds of groups and ask people to put their post-it notes on the appropriate section and to explain them to the group.	Tutor Prompt Sheet 7 Prepared continuum, post-it notes	
1.10	What are the issues we need to consider when thinking about community groups?	Small groups to quick flip ideas which will be collated and used to ensure the topics are covered during the course	Tutor Prompt Sheet 8	
1.20	Why do people join groups? Expectations and motivations	People to interview three or four other people about their own motivation for, and expectations of, joining a group. Tutor to summarise	Tutor Prompt Sheet 9 Worksheet 1	
1.45	Reflective journals (RJ)	Give out RJ questions and remind people of what's required	Reflective Journal 1	
1.50	Ending exercise			
2.00	End			

Life cycle of groups

Give out Handout 4. This is the handout used in the Community Development Work Skills course. If participants have completed that course you can remind them of the section on the life cycle of groups, if they have not been on this course then you can introduce the idea that groups tend to have a similar life cycle.

Using buzz groups (these can either be pairs or trios, and to form them you say 'turn to your neighbour(s) and discuss ...'.

Using their own experience of groups they should make a list of the ups and downs of the groups they have been involved in and put them into a rough chronological order – which experiences related to early in a group's life, what was going on in its active phase and what was occurring towards the end of the group's life.

The aim is to get them to think of a couple of things in each phase.

Ask the buzz groups to feed back their ideas. You can then relate these to one of the models on Handout 4.

Open up a whole group discussion of what are the implications of knowing this for their work as community development workers/activists.

The main points to draw out are that:

◆ Each stage will require a different role from the worker, for example, at the beginning you may be more of a leader, in difficult times more of a facilitator/mediator

◆ The stage of the group will affect what it is able to achieve. If it is busy trying to sort out its internal dynamics then it may not produce much external activity which your funders may be looking to you to ensure the group delivers

◆ You may have been asked to work with the group to sort out its dynamics and you may be seen as siding with one part of the group against another. You don't tend to be asked to work with fully functioning groups

◆ If you are not involved from the beginning you may not understand the tensions, the history, the aspirations, and so on. Sometimes it is good to know these things and sometimes it is good to be outside all of it.

The life cycle of groups

All groups go through different stages as they grow and develop. When it feels heavy going it is worth thinking about where the group has got to in its cycle as that can help you decide what to do and whether you should worry about it.

◆ People come together because they want to change something and they cannot do it on their own

◆ The group gets together and people want it to work and they assume that everyone is thinking the same

◆ As the group members work together so they find that they have very different expectations and tensions can begin to rise and arguments occur

◆ The group members want to make it work and so try and clarify what the group is there for. There may be competing and conflicting demands on the group

◆ Some people might leave and others carry on as they are a bit more realistic about what can be achieved, and they start to achieve some of their goals

◆ Conflict surfaces again – it seems hard again and some people just want to give up. It seems hard to achieve anything and people cling to old ways of working

◆ Suddenly it seems to work again, people go with the flow of the group and there is more energy and the group works well together and begins to achieve again

◆ The group achieves most of its aims and there is a sense that its time has come. People start to think of a life beyond this group; some people leave and a few may move onto other groups or actions. It is a time of celebration and sadness.

This view of groups is that they go up and down – like a roller coaster. There are other ways of looking at groups which tend to be more linear; here are four examples:

1 Tubbs's Small Group Development Theory has four stages:

Orientation   In this stage, group members get to know each other, they start to talk about the problem, and they examine the limitations and opportunities of the project

Conflict   Conflict is a necessary part of a group's development. Conflict allows the group to evaluate ideas and it helps the group avoid conformity and groupthink

Consensus   Conflict ends in the consensus stage, when group members compromise, select ideas and agree on alternatives

Closure   In this stage, the final result is announced and group members reaffirm their support of the decision.

2 Fisher's Small Group Development Theory – again 4 stages:

Orientation   During the orientation phase, Fisher says group members get to know each other and they experience primary tension, the awkward feeling people have before communication rules and expectations are established. Groups should take time to learn about each other and feel comfortable communicating around new people

Conflict   The conflict phase is marked by secondary tension, or tension surrounding the task at hand. Group members will disagree with each other and debate ideas. Remember that conflict is good, because it helps the group achieve positive results

Emergence   In the emergence phase the outcome of the group's task and its social structure become apparent

Reinforcement   In this stage, group members bolster their final decision by using supportive verbal and nonverbal communication.

❸ Tuckman's Small Group Development Theory – you may well have heard of this one as it's quite a popular model:

Forming   In the forming stage, group members learn about each other and the task at hand

Storming   As group members become more comfortable with each other, they will engage each other in arguments and vie for status in the group. These activities mark the storming phase

Norming   During the norming stage, group members establish implicit or explicit rules about how they will achieve their goal. They address the types of communication that will or will not help with the task

Performing   In the performing stage, groups reach a conclusion and implement the conclusion

Adjourning   As the group project ends, the group disbands in the adjournment phase. This stage is sometimes called **the mourning stage** as people say goodbye to each other and to the group.

Other writers have felt that these models are too simplistic and so here is one which tries to explain the complexities of group life:

❹ Poole's Small Group Development Theory:

Task track   Marshall Scott Poole and his colleagues have found that group development is often more complicated than the three previous models indicate. He has argued that groups jump back and forth between three tracks: task, topic, and relation. The three tracks can be compared to the intertwined strands of a rope. The task track concerns the process by which the group accomplishes its goals

Topic track   The topic track concerns the specific item the group is discussing at the time

Relation track   The relation track deals with the interpersonal relationships between the group members. At times, the group may stop its work on the task and work instead on its relationships. When the group reaches consensus on all three tracks at once, it can proceed in a more unified manner as the three previous models illustrate

Breakpoints   Breakpoints occur when a group switches from one track to another. Shifts in the conversation, adjournment, or postponement are examples of breakpoints.

The range of groups in the community and voluntary sectors

The aim of this exercise if to get people to appreciate the wide range of groups within the voluntary and community sectors.

Give everyone a few post-it notes and ask them to write down the names of different groups they are involved in or know enough about to be able to put them into a category.

You need to put several pieces of flip chart paper together and draw a continuum along the bottom and put the different types of groups along this continuum.

The range of group headings could include:

- Self-help groups
- Community care groups
- Community activity groups
- Community organising groups
- Campaigning groups
- Community enterprise groups

- Neighbourhood based associations
- Social planning groups
- Community of interest groups
- Community centres/village halls
- Political groups
- Community action groups.

Or you can use the different kinds of legal status:

- Small groups with no constitution
- Unincorporated community groups with a constitution
- Small charities registered with the charity commission
- Larger charities registered with both the Charity Commission and Company's House

- Companies limited by guarantee
- Not-for-profit community businesses
- Community Foundations
- Community Development Trusts.

Ask group members to put their post-it notes against the relevant section. If you have a large and mobile group you can use the floor and make a continuum with masking tape and get people to stand along the continuum and explain their groups.

Issues within community groups

The aim of this exercise is to give course members another chance to raise issues that could be covered on this course.

Form people into small groups to quick flip the issues they think need to be considered when working with a community group. This can be taken in quite a broad way and hopefully it will get them thinking about what they need to consider when approaching group work.

Pin the flip charts up and let people read them, and then move onto the next exercise. You will use the information to ensure that all their concerns are covered in this course and to help customise exercises or your input.

Motivations and expectation

Give out Worksheet 1 and ask people to interview three to four people each and find out why they joined a particular group and what they hoped to gain from this.

Ask them to summarise in their feedback the main motivations that people expressed and log this onto a flip chart.

There should be a range of motivations from those who are motivated by something quite personal through to more altruistic aspects.

Motivations can include some of the following:

◆ Need for help with a particular problem such as getting housing repairs done

◆ To get support during a particular crisis or hard time such as carers support group

◆ To give something back to a group that helped them through a bad patch

◆ To do something positive for their families and their friends such as organising a Saturday football league for children

◆ To respond to an event in their neighbourhood, for example, a child being knocked down on the street and a campaign for lower speed limits or road calming

◆ To make sure that important aspects of their culture are not lost, such as Saturday Schools on African or Albanian culture, history and language

◆ To preserve something of importance such as stopping a road or housing development through a local woodland

◆ To gain support from, and show solidarity with, others over a big issue, such as stopping a war or nuclear weapons or the destruction of the rain forests.

Why do people join groups?

Using the grid below interview three or four people on the course and find out what groups they joined and why and what they hoped to achieve.

Their name	A group they joined	Why they joined it	What did they expect to gain by joining the group

Group Work Skills • **Session Two**
Federation for Community Development Learning

Reflective Journal

To be completed after each 4 hours of group work

Name of participant _____

Name of Tutor/s _____

1 Give a brief description of the topics covered by the group work and highlight your main areas of learning.

2 What did you think and feel about the group? What did you contribute to the group and its work?

3 Did you find anything difficult in the session and/or are there areas you would like us to cover again?

Portfolio question

You need to demonstrate an understanding of the reasons why people become involved in community groups and networks.

For level 2 you should describe the range of motivations and expectations that people might have when joining a community group or network. Give some examples of different groups or networks to illustrate different motivations.

For level 3 you should analyse in some detail the reasons for people joining a particular group and discuss the implications these motivations and expectations can have for the group or network.

(Complete during the week)

Make notes of anything or thoughts that have occurred during the week which you feel challenged you, or re-emphasised your beliefs/experiences.

Tutor's comments

Signature of participant _____

Signature of tutor/s _____ Date _____

Group dynamics and conflict in groups

Group dynamics and conflict in groups
Session Plan 3 and 4

◆ **Target audience**

People involved in and working with community groups

◆ **Length of session**

2 x 2-hour sessions; four hours in total

◆ **Session aim(s)**

● To explore some of the theories around group dynamics and conflicts in groups

◆ **Session outcomes**

At the end of the session students/trainees will...

● **Level 2:** Demonstrate a understanding of group dynamics and the potential for conflict to arise

● **Level 3:** Demonstrate a understanding of group work theory and the potential for conflict to arise in groups/networks

◆ **Indicative content**

● Theories of groups

● Group dynamics

● Power relationships; change; structures – and their impact on group dynamics

● Causes of conflict

● Approaches to tackling conflict

● Using conflict creatively to bring about change.

Detailed Session Plan 3

Time	Content	Exercise/Method	Resources	Notes core topic or optional if time
0.00	Warm up game			
0.15	Admin; any OCN forms; collect in Reflective Journals	Tutor input		
0.20	Recap on last week; aims of this week	Tutor input	Tutor Prompt Sheet 10	
0.20	What do we know about groups and how they work?	Individuals to think about what they have come across. Tutor to note on flip chart	Tutor Prompt Sheet 10	
0.35	What do we mean by group dynamics?	Split into groups of three or four to note down key words and make into a phrase or statement	Tutor Prompt Sheet 10	
0.55	Key factors affecting the dynamics within a group	Small groups to discuss groups they have been in and to try and isolate the main factors which affected whether the group worked well or not	Tutor Prompt Sheet 11	
1.20	Where can conflict arise within groups	Small groups to construct a group which has all kind of conflicts built into it. They should make a list of everything that can go wrong and choose one or two scenes to act out/mime to the rest of the group	Tutor Prompt Sheet 12	
2.00	End			

Aims of the session

Recap – remind the group that in the last sessions they have been looking at the overview of issues around community groups and begun to explore people's motivations for joining groups.

The aims of sessions 3 and 4 are to explore the theories that help us explain what is happening in groups, what we can call group dynamics and to look at ways of tackling conflict within groups

The first exercise is to ascertain what group members know about groups and group dynamics. Ask individuals to think about anything they have heard about, read about, been on training about on the topic of group dynamics. Log up anything they can contribute – explain that its not important if they haven't but that you want to gauge their level of knowledge so that you pitch the course at the right level.

The second exercise is to agree on what we mean by group dynamics. Get people into groups of three or four to note down the key words for them about group dynamics and to try and make a sentence or phrase using these words.

Feedback and record the different statements and words, summarise into an agreement about what we are talking about.

Key factors affecting group dynamics

Split the participants into small groups and ask them to think about groups they have been involved in, either in the past or currently. Ask them to pull out some of the main factors that affected the way the group worked.

You could give some examples such as:

◆ The group being chaired by a local politician who tried to prevent the group making any criticisms of the local authority (power issues)

◆ A major grant coming to an end and lack of alternative funding (a resourcing issue)

◆ All the correspondence going to the secretary who never passed on information in time for people to go to events they group were invited to (communication)

◆ One of the members always coming late and having to leave early (behaviour)

◆ Whenever the group starts to argue or debate fiercely someone always suggests a break and makes tea (informal rules).

The aim of this exercise is to get people to think about what goes on within groups. When taking the feedback you could try to cluster the different factors. You may have sub-headings of:

Power – in all its different forms

Change – externally imposed and internally generated

Structures – formal and informal systems which can create barriers of communication and decision-making

Relationships – between people in the group and between group members and outsiders.

Conflict within groups

Divide the participants into two or three reasonably sized groups.

Their task is to create the group with the most amount of conflict possible.

Their first task is to list all the types of conflicts that they can think of and put them on post-it notes. Their second task is to choose one or two scenes from this list and act them out or mime them to the whole group as part of the feedback. The watching groups have to guess what is going on.

The feedback is in two parts:

◆ first, the role plays/mimes

◆ second, the collection of all the post-it notes, which should be grouped into similar categories on the flip charts.

This should provide a light-hearted way of raising where conflicts can occur within a group.

Detailed Session Plan 4

Time	Content	Exercise/Method	Resources	Notes *core topic or optional if time*
0.00	Wake up game			
0.10	Understanding the causes of conflicts	Scenarios on conflict situations	Tutor Prompt Sheet 13 Worksheet 2	
0.40	Different approaches to tackling conflict – how do they respond?	When faced with a conflict in a group what is their reaction – draw or mime. Tutor to summarise reactions	Tutor Prompt Sheet 14 Handout 5	
1.00	Creative approaches to tackling conflict	Tutor input on different models; application to scenarios in small groups or large group to use the Playing with Fire model	Tutor Prompt Sheet 15 Handout 6 and 7	
1.45	Reflective journal – give out questions; return marked journals		Reflective Journal 2	
1.50	Ending exercise			
2.00	End			

Understanding the causes of conflict

The aim of this exercise is to get people to look beyond the surface and to think what might be behind conflicts within groups.

Organise people into small groups and give each one a case study. You can either use some of your own or those arising within the group or those below. There is a worksheet which can be used by people in their groups to record their thoughts.

■ Case study 1

As a new community development worker in an area you have been asked to attend a meeting of an active group of older people. When you get there, two of the group members take the lead and they tell you that they have been awarded a small grant to set up a luncheon club and they want to know how to go about setting it up. You pick up some vibes that not all is well. As you ask the other people to introduce themselves you find out that not everyone knew about the grant being applied for and that actually they don't want a luncheon club. They are fed up with being stereotyped and some say they would rather have an evening disco for the over-70s. The two people who had started to take the lead say that most people are with them and that there are just a few trouble-makers who are trying to turn people against them.

■ Case study 2

You are a community development worker supporting a group of people on an estate who meet weekly to undertake craft activities. For some of them this is the only time that they can get out of the house with the permission of their partners and families, as this group is seen as safe. The group is important to many of the women who attend, as it provides time away from their families and acts as an informal advice and guidance session for them. One of the women, who used to go out more and has a history of being involved in community groups, finds that her personal circumstances change when her husband retires and he is now in the house all day. This effectively curtails her freedom to go out and about. The effect of this comes out in the group with long angry tirades, and by an increased intrusiveness into the lives of the other women. Many of the other women are saying that they will no longer attend if this woman continues to behave in this way.

■ Case study 3

A few years ago some parents of Learning Disabled people set up their own organisation. They obtained a house in the countryside and started to do it up for workshops, social activities and holidays. The organisation grew in numbers and started to do some work with other Disabled people's organisations and with their help they managed to get some funding for a worker. This worker's main job was to support a small number of the Learning Disabled people to move towards independent living. As the group developed, important issues began to arise such as the Learning Disabled people not being able to open their own bank account or the way that the day centre staff treated them. The worker set about tackling some of these problems and in the process had a number of arguments with officials and professionals. At the same time some of the group members began to take seriously this idea of living independently or at least changing the way they lived within their families. Some parents found this hard to accept as they didn't like the idea of their 'children' becoming independent and not using the segregated provision at the house. All of this led to big debates within the management committee about the worker and her role and whether they should sack her or support her.

■ Case study 4

A residents group has been running for a few years as an entirely voluntary group, taking up local issues with the councillors and organising clean up campaigns and local events to bring the community together. Their area has been targeted to become a regeneration area. At one meeting this is discussed and the chair and secretary agree to go off to a fact finding meeting with the local authority and report back. At the next meeting they report that they have signed up for a funding bid of £150,000 to get workers and some money for local improvements. The group's current budget is £3,000. They argue that unless they had done this they would have been left out as the deadline was quite close and the council officers were offering to help. Others feel that the group will be changed too much into an organisation rather than a grass roots group.

Understanding the causes of conflict

Your scenario ....

(write in details or attach the case study)

Make a list of all the possible causes of conflict within this scenario and say what you think has led to this situation developing.

Different responses to conflict

The aim of this exercise is to get people to think about the range of different ways that people react to conflict. Some people love conflict and really thrive in those situations. Others really hate it and will do anything to avoid it, some will try and hide conflict, others will try and bring things out into the open.

Ask each person to think of a conflict situation – and these can be quite small events such as not wanting to baby-sit for your friend that night, or to deliver some leaflets for the community gala, as well as the larger events.

If some people can't think of any conflicts then give them a small scenario such as asking them to stay behind today and wash all the dishes up from the group's lunch.

Ask them to decide how they could mime how they reacted. Give them two to three minutes to think and then go round and ask them to say what the conflict was and to mime their reaction. The group will guess what their response was and you will note these on a flip chart.

At the end of this round, summarise by explaining that we all react to conflict in different ways. We need to be aware of this when we are trying to resolve conflicts in our community groups and networks.

Conflict management approaches – part 1

Approach	Objective	Your posture	Supporting rationale	Likely outcome
Forcing	Get your way	I know what is right. Don't question my authority	It is better to risk causing a few hard feelings than to abandon the issue	You feel vindicated but the other party feels defeated and possibly humiliated
Avoiding	Avoid having to deal with conflict	I'm neutral on that issue. Let me think about it. That's someone else's problem	Disagreements are inherently bad because they create tension	Interpersonal problems don't get resolved causing long term frustration manifested in many ways
Compromising	Reach an agreement quickly	Let's search for a solution that we can both live with so we can get on with our work	Prolonged conflicts distract people from their work and cause bitter feelings	Participants go for the expedient rather than effective solutions
Accommodating	Don't upset the other person	How can I help you to feel good about this? My position is not so important that it is worth risking bad feelings between us	Maintaining harmonious relationships should be our top priority	The other person is likely to take advantage
Collaborating	Solve the problem together	This is my position, what is yours? I'm committed to finding the best solution. What do the facts suggest?	Each position is important though not necessarily equally valid. Emphasis should be put on the quality of the outcome and the fairness of the decision-making process	The problem is most likely to be resolved. Also both parties are committed to the solution and satisfied that they have been treated fairly

From Developing Management Skills for Europe Whetton,
Cameron, Woods Harper Collins 1994

Conflict management approaches – part 2

Styles of Conflict Management – Researchers Ruble and Thomas have identified five styles for managing conflict. The styles can be charted on two dimensions: assertiveness and cooperativeness.

Style	Assertiveness	Co-operativeness
Competitive	High Competitive people want to win the conflict.	Low
Accommodative	Low	High These group members are easy going and willing to follow the group.
Avoiding	Low	Low Avoiding people are detached and indifferent to conflict.
Collaborative	High	High These group members are active and productive problem solvers.
Compromising	Moderate	Moderate Compromisers are willing to 'give and take' to resolve conflict.

Creative approaches to conflict

Introduce the idea that conflict is not unhealthy and can be used in a positive manner (Handout 7) and that what is needed is to get the conditions right and to manage the situation (Handout 6 and 7).

Using the different models you can ask the groups to look again at scenarios they worked on earlier and ask them to think about which approach they would take and how they would approach handling the situation.

Another method you can use is to take the key words from the Playing With Fire model (Handout 7). Make them into large sheets and ideally laminate them. Put them on the floor in a circle and ask people to stand behind each word in turn and to discuss a common conflict, such as a recent war, demonstration, or fight. You can then work through one of their conflicts or one of the scenarios in the same way.

Getting the climate right to manage conflict

Defensive climate

The climate in which conflict is managed is important. Groups should avoid a defensive climate which is characterised by these qualities:

◆ Evaluation: judging and criticising other group members

◆ Control: imposing the will of one group member on the others

◆ Strategy: using hidden agendas.

◆ Neutrality: demonstrating indifference and lack of commitment

◆ Superiority: expressing dominance

◆ Certainty: being rigid in one's willingness to listen to others.

Supportive Climate

Instead, groups should foster a supportive climate, marked by these traits:

◆ Description: presenting ideas or opinions

◆ Problem orientation: focusing attention on the task

◆ Spontaneity: communicating openly and honestly

◆ Empathy: understanding another person's thoughts

◆ Equality: asking for opinions

◆ Provisionalism: expressing a willingness to listen to the ideas of others.

Conflict in Groups

Conflict should not always be seen as a negative, it can often be used to bring about helpful change and to unblock groups which have got stuck. Burying conflict doesn't mean that it goes away, it just means that you don't know when and how it will burst out again – often in quite strange ways and in unpredictable circumstances. Many writers suggest that conflict can be good for a group if it is managed appropriately. It is often better to try and manage the conflict and use it positively even though it might seem very hard and dangerous at the time. By airing their differences, group members can produce quality decisions and also develop and satisfy their interpersonal relationships.

The first step in managing conflict is to identify the conflict – to know what it is all about and what is behind it. For example:

◆   Do the group members know that a conflict exists?

◆   Are the group members arguing over competing goals?

◆   Are scarce resources at stake?

◆   Are the group members dependent on each other to solve the conflict?

Playing with Fire

One model that many people have found useful is that developed by Nic Fine and Fiona Macbeth called *Playing With Fire*. Produced by Leap, it is published by the Youth Work Press, The National Youth Agency.

The model is outlined on the back of this handout and it is one which is easy to understand – we know that huge fires in different parts of the world seem at first to be highly devastating but they are also nature's way of clearing out all the dead wood and undergrowth and that from the burnt land all sorts of other plants start to grow – some of them are only able to grow when their seeds have been heated so fiercely that their shells can crack.

Conflict	Fire	Change
People Whenever people are in contact with each other, there is potential for conflict. This potential will vary according to the different degrees of combustibility in the individuals.	**The Fuel** The raw material of the fire. Some of it is highly combustible. Some of it is damp and flame resistant.	**People** Whenever people are in contact with each other, there is potential for challenge and growth. Different values, opinions or aims contain raw issues and fuel for fire.
Incident There are always tensions and disagreements between people. Some of them can cause a spark, which ignites conflict.	**The Spark** Friction causes sparks to fly. Some land on dry wood and it catches alight.	**Flash of Insight** There are always raw issues in a community or relationship. Sometimes a flash of new insight can bring an issue alive for an individual.
Brooding Tensions and grievances are smouldering away but are unexpressed. The conflict feeds off rumour and gossip.	**Smouldering** The fuel catches alight and begins to smoke. There is an indication of fire.	**Tentative Response** The individual looks for shared concern from others, making an initial response to the issue.
Aggravation Those who are interested in agitating the situation provoke it further. Feelings of anger and hurt may be expressed as prejudice and hate.	**Fanning the Flames** The wind blows and the smouldering fuel flickers with life. The flames lick and leap.	**Encouraged Action** Those showing concern for the issue grow in number, encouraging and supporting each other.
Escalation The situation is intensified by the outside pressures of the social environment. Prejudice and disaffection add to the conflict.	**Stoking the Fire** The fire consumes the fuel. It demands more. Huge logs are piled onto the fire.	**Increased Response** Response to the issue increases. The possibilities of achievement inspire action from many.
Consequences There is a blazing conflict in which some people are damaged. No-one involved is untouched by it.	**The Blaze** The fire rages. It is a huge blaze. It will not die down easily.	**Effective Action** Aims are achieved. People celebrate the blazing fire. It is a beacon which lights, warms and inspires.

Reflective Journal

To be completed after each 4 hours of group work

Name of participant _____

Name of Tutor/s _____

1 Give a brief description of the topics covered by the group work and highlight your main areas of learning.

2 What did you think and feel about the group? What did you contribute to the group and its work?

3 Did you find anything difficult in the session and/or are there areas you would like us to cover again?

Portfolio question

You need to demonstrate an understanding of group dynamics and the potential for conflict to arise.

For level 2 you should:

1. Describe the group dynamics of a group that you know

2. Suggest how the conflict(s) in this (or another) group could be defused or handled effectively.

For level 3 you should:

1. Describe a group and explain its life cycle and where it is at the present time

2. Using examples, analyse the most likely causes of tensions within community groups and networks and suggest how they could best be defused or managed to help the group achieve its aims.

(Complete during the week)

Make notes of anything or thoughts that have occurred during the week which you feel challenged you, or re-emphasised your beliefs/experiences.

Tutor's comments

Signature of participant _____

Signature of tutor/s _____ Date _____

Setting up a group

Setting up a group
Session Plan 5 and 6

◆ **Target audience**

People involved in and working with community groups

◆ **Length of session**

2 x 2-hour sessions; four hours in total

◆ **Session aim(s)**

● To look at the issues involved in setting up a group

◆ **Session outcomes**

At the end of the session students/trainees will…

● Demonstrate an understanding of processes involved when a group/network sets its objectives and priorities

◆ **Indicative content**

● Initiating a group

● Understanding the history of groups in the area and local context

● Is the group really needed?

● Deciding on the vision, the aim

● Setting group objectives and priorities

● Using people's skills within a group

● How to organise effectively as a group

● Structures – what to suggest, options to meet the objectives of the group

● Helping groups to change over time; reviewing progress, replanning

Detailed Session Plan 5

Time	Content	Exercise/Method	Resources	Notes *core topic or optional if time*
0.00	Warm up			
0.15	Admin – collect in journals Aims	Tutor to recap on past sessions and to introduce aim of today about setting up a new group	Tutor input	The ideal is to set up a group in such a way as to avoid conflict being built in
0.20	Issues around setting up a group/network	Small groups to look at scenario and produce checklist	Tutor Prompt Sheet 16 Worksheet 3	
0.40	Bringing people together to develop a shared vision	Case study for two groups	Tutor Prompt Sheet 17 Worksheet 4	
1.05	Setting up the aims of a group or network. Assessing the resources needed and what is within the group	Tutor input with story. Continue case study in smaller groups. Feedback	Tutor Prompt Sheet 18 Worksheet 5	
2.00	End			

Group Work Skills • **Session Five**
Federation for Community Development Learning

Setting up a new group

The aim of this exercise is to get people to think widely around the idea of setting up a new group and whether it is actually needed.

Give out Worksheet 3 with the scenario and ask small groups to come up with their checklist. Some of the answers that you would expect would include:

◆ Understanding the history of the area

◆ Uunderstanding the context in which the group will be working – social, economic, political

◆ Other groups and networks that might be doing the same or similar things

◆ The need for this new group, could another group take on this work?

◆ Rights and responsibilities of groups

◆ Needs and opportunities for the group at this time

◆ What type of group is being planned – is it appropriate?

◆ Who wants it? Why?

◆ Why is a group is the best way forward?

◆ Is there enough support for it?

◆ Is it a short-term group, a long-term group?

◆ Does it have clear aims?

◆ How will it link into other groups/networks/organisations?

◆ Will it meet together in person, through telephone or e-mail?

Summarise by saying that it is important that people coming together do start to develop a shared vision which will see them through the difficult times ahead.

Developing a new group

You have won the main lottery prize of several million pounds and have decided to set up your own local trust fund to give money to local groups which are just starting up.

Develop a checklist of all the points that you would expect any newly starting group to have thought about. It might include, what is the need? what type of group would be best? is it right for the area?

Our checklist

1

2

3

4

5

6

7

8

9

10

Developing a new group – part 1

The aim of this exercise is to get people to think about creating an inclusive and diverse group right from the start. The participants should be encouraged to think about different participatory approaches that could be used to bring people together. You could start with a quick round of what people know about different approaches, for example using roundtable discussions, vision techniques, drawing exercises. The important point to make is that public meetings held in the traditional manner are not likely to engage people effectively. More information about ways to engage people will be found in the 'Involving People' Resource Pack.

The case study is deliberately vague and wide open to interpretation. The group has to work out how to define the focus of the group using their own experiences – health has been chosen because it affects everyone.

Split the group into two reasonably sized groups, or if it is a smallish group let them work as a whole group. Give them the task on Worksheet 4.

Ask them to feedback on flip charts so that the different approaches can be seen.

Developing a health group

You have been given the task of pulling together a community based group which will look at the health needs of people living in the area served by a large health centre. The area is very mixed with different housing types, different social classes and half-a-dozen different ethnic communities.

Health is being defined very widely and can include everything from the environment, healthy living, getting better services from local Health Centres and Hospitals.

◆ For the purpose of this exercise you live in this area and you represent your own health needs and interests.

◆ As a group of diverse people, decide how would you plan to bring people together to develop a shared idea of what the group could be about.

◆ You need to discuss the different participatory approaches that can be used and decide which is most appropriate.

◆ Who would you need to make sure was there?

Developing a new group – part 2

Tell the story

'A person entering a new group is like a stranger in a darkened room. The first thing they do is to try and find the light switch. They grope around and decide that it is safest to follow the wall. In doing so they stumble against a low table. This alarms them and they realise their plan is not foolproof. A number of doubts arise, raising questions such as 'what will I walk into next?' Anxieties begin to mount up. Past experiences and previous assumptions all fail them. They wonder if someone is playing tricks. Will they ever reach the light?

Indeed! Would any of us put in the role of the stranger in a darkened room react differently. Some might kick vigorously at the table; others might call for help; some would sit down in a corner and wait for someone else to find the light switch. Others might experiment by looking for a box of matches on the table. Others might simply leave the house.'

Invite comments

Make the following points:

◆ It is inevitable that problems will arise as we start new groups, but we can see this as an opportunity rather than as a calamity as it gives us the opportunity to work out the best way to work together.

◆ Anyone entering a new group brings with them a certain amount of baggage – based on previous situations and experiences. They tend to have certain expectations about the new situation and to make certain assumptions regarding it. These can arise from:

  ❖ Their concept of themselves and others

  ❖ Their understanding of patterns of leadership

  ❖ Authority structures

  ❖ Operating procedures.

◆ The baggage they bring with them will affect how they behave in the new situation so it is important to explore people's experiences and expectations when forming a new group. Some of the key questions are:

  ❖ Why am I here?

  ❖ Who am I here? (what hat have I on?)

  ❖ Why are you here?

  ❖ How should I behave here?

If we explore some of these questions then the level of ambiguity and uncertainty can be reduced which will help a group to gel more readily.

Then ask the group to split into smaller groups. Ask them to decide how they would go about establishing the aims of the health group or network. They need to take into account the points about using what people bring with them in terms of experiences, expectations and assumptions.

Ask them first to look at how to establish the aim(s) of the group and to record this. Then they should think about the resources they would need to be able to develop the group or network beyond this first stage. Resources could include:

◆   The skills of members of the group at being in a group

◆   The expertise they bring around health issues

◆   Access to physical resources – paper/stamps/telephones

◆   And so on…

The group should then decide what resources it needs and how it will find out if it has them.

Setting the aims of the group or network

The aim of a group is a broad statement or statements about what the group wants to do.

In your group continue to talk about the health group or network you have been asked to develop. People have come together to share some ideas about what they would like the group to be about, now you have to turn this into an agreement about the actual aims of the group so people know what the group is about.

1 Decide how you will go about setting the aims to make the most of people's expertise, experiences, interests and skills.

2 Now agree on an aim for your group.

3 What resources will you need to get this group moving? How will you find out what already exists in the group?

Detailed Session Plan 6

Time	Content	Exercise/Method	Resources	Notes core topic or optional if time
0.00	Wake up			
0.10	Establishing objectives and priorities	Tutor input on what is meant by objectives and the different ways to set them and prioritise them Groups to reconvene to establish objectives for their health group/ network	Tutor Prompt Sheet 19 Handout 8	
1.05	Different organisational structures to meet objectives	Tutor input on different organisational structures. Small groups to consider what is best for particular groups/ networks	Tutor Prompt Sheet 20 Handout 9 Worksheet 6	
1.35	Building in reviews, monitoring and evaluation of group	Tutor input on the action reflection cycle. Whole group work	Tutor Prompt Sheet 21 Handout 10	
1.45	Reflective Journals and ending game	Hand out the journal sheets	Reflective Journal 3	
2.00	End			

Establishing objectives and priorities

Remind the group that they have set their aims for their health group/network and that the aim(s) were fairly broad statements about what they wanted to achieve. Aims can be seen as strategic statements.

Objectives are statements about how they intend to achieve their aim(s), they are operational statements about the group/project. Objectives need to be clearly written and straightforward so that people can understand them and it is easy to see if they are being achieved.

One way of writing objectives is using the SMART approach. Use Handout 8 to explain this approach to people. Ask the groups to reconvene and to work out three or four objectives for their health group or network.

When they have fed back their ideas you then need to talk about how groups/networks can prioritise their objectives. Some of the common techniques involve time line approaches such as:

◆ now, sooner, later

◆ short-term, medium-term, longer-term.

You can draw these out on a flip chart to explain how these work – the group makes a list of tasks for each objective (using post-it notes is an easy way). These are then located onto the timeline with the discussion of the whole group.

Other techniques involve ranking the importance of the objectives, and for this the group can use techniques such as:

◆ The Disagree game (see handout from Community Development Work Skills Resource Pack)

◆ Red spots (the objectives are listed on a flip chart and each person is given a number of red spot labels to allocate to the objectives they rank highest – the objectives receiving the highest number of red spots become the priority objectives).

You can explain that there are many different ways of setting priorities and invite participants to share any other ideas.

SMART objectives

The objectives of an organisation, group or project follow on from its vision and its aims. They explain how the group will achieve its aim(s). They need to be clearly written and quite straightforward so that people can understand them and it is easy to see if they are being achieved. One method of writing objectives is to use the heading of SMART.

S pecific — They are to the point, they are not complicated and do not include multiple tasks

M easurable — They should be written so that it is clear when the objectives have been reached

A ttainable — They should be achievable by the group/network

R elevant — They should relate to the purpose of the group/network

T imed — They should be able to fit into a sensible time scale and an action plan.

Once objectives have been written they need to be agreed by the group members and put into priority order. The tasks then need to be shared out so that people are clear who has agreed to do what and by when – this forms the basis of an action plan for the group.

Organisational structure

There are many different forms of organisations that groups can choose to take; the form they choose should be relevant to the work they want to undertake. There is always a danger that inappropriate structures are imposed upon groups when they start up. This is often about other organisations' agendas rather then the needs of a group. For example, partnerships being expected to be companies limited by guarantee, or funders wanting charitable status.

Give out Handout 19. Use the handout to explain the different structures available to new groups and how they can change over time to suit the needs of the group or organisation.

Put people into groups of three and give out Worksheet 6 and ask them to complete it.

Different organisational structures

Informal group/network – where a few people come together to achieve a goal – for example, a response to a threat to build on some open space – and they want to act quickly to achieve their aim. They do not have any rules and they do not register with any body. Another example could be a self-help group – a number of people who meet to walk every day around their local park as part of their recovery from a heart attack.

An unincorporated association – where a group has short term goals and no, or very little, income. They may agree a basic set of rules so that they can work together to achieve their aim.

An unincorporated charity – if a group has an income of more than £1000 per year and its aims are considered to be charitable, then the group must apply for charitable status and adopt a constitution that is acceptable to the Charity Commissioners. The Commissioners require all charities with an income of over £10,000 to send in their annual accounts. There are different requirements depending on the charity's income. Registration gives an organisation a charity number which often helps with fund-raising, but also limits the freedom of an organisation to campaign and to trade.

All of the above structures treat the group as a collection of individuals who are jointly and separately liable for the groups obligations and debts.
So, individuals can become liable for the debts incurred by a group. Any property will have to be held in individual's names and any legal proceedings have to be taken by individuals.

Company limited by guarantee – these are companies recognised in law as a legal body, they are usually found in the voluntary sector because any profits must be put back into the company for the good of the company and not taken as dividends by share holders. Members pay a small fee, often £1, and that is the extent of their liability in case anything goes wrong, provided that they haven't made unjustifiable decisions – like spending money they know they haven't got!

A company exists in law in its own right and so it can buy property, protect its members, initiate legal proceedings etc. It has to send its annual accounts to Companies House each year and to keep them informed of all its Directors whose details are listed and publicly available (anyone needing to keep their address secret cannot become a Director, for example if a woman fleeing domestic abuse wanted to help run the local refuge by joining the board they would not be able to keep their address secret and so may be tracked by a violent ex-partner through these lists.)

Charitable Companies – companies limited by guarantee can apply to the Charity Commission to become charities as well. At the moment this requires an organisation to register with Companies House and with the Charity Commission and report to both; the current review of charity law may make this process easier.

Incorporation is usually considered by those organisations with a reasonable turnover (a rule of thumb is around £125,000) and with staff and premises.

There can be quite high costs associated with becoming an incorporated body, and higher levels of accountability are demanded by the regulating bodies.

The key points to consider when trying to decide what structure to start with:

◆ Risk

◆ Set-up costs

◆ Need for charity number

◆ Desire to campaign

◆ Desire to trade

◆ Privacy

◆ Accountability to members.

As groups grow into organisations and take on more responsibilities so they can change their structure to suit their new situation.

The book *Voluntary But Not Amateur* has excellent chapters on looking at the advantages and disadvantages of each form of organisation. It is available from LVSC, 356 Holloway Road London N7 6PA.
Tel: 020 7700 8107. Email: info@lvsc.org.uk or web: www.lvsc.org.uk

The Charity Commission web site is very helpful www.charity-commission.gov.uk and the commission runs an excellent help line 0870 333 0123.

This is a very brief outline of the different possibilities available to groups and you should always seek further advice before committing a group to any one course of action. There are pros and cons for every structure and the people involved will need to fully understand their responsibilities and protection for each one.

Most community groups do not have staff or their own premises and therefore they do not need elaborate and over complex structures imposed on them. Encourage the group to start with what is appropriate for now and which they can feel comfortable with. They can always change later when they have more resources to meet the demands of regulatory bodies.

Organisational structure

Which type of organisational structure is likely to be relevant to the following groups emerging from your work on health issues?

A 'walking bus' to get children walking to school, run by volunteer parents taking it in turns	
A self-help group for Asian people with diabetes	
A campaigning group to get the local chemical factory to reduce its noxious emissions	
A Healthy Living Centre project to build a new centre with staff	
A fund-raising group to get a new scanner for the local hospital	
Awareness raising around drugs issues within different communities	

Reviewing the group's development

The aim of this slot is to introduce the concept of learning from practice, by reflecting on what a group has done and what it needs to do in future.

Input

Using Handout 10 explain how the action reflection cycle works.

Discuss the importance of a group/network regularly reviewing its progress against its initial objectives. Groups change quite quickly and can encounter difficulties early in their life (refer to the earlier session) and so it is important that they regularly build in time to look at what they are doing and if they need to replan because of a changing situation. For example, new opportunities have arisen or their original objective cannot be realised, or not yet.

Exercise

In the whole group, use the examples of the different types of health groups/networks that the small groups decided to establish earlier on. Ask the whole group to consider how they would build in reviews and monitor the group's objectives.

The issues they need to consider are:

◆   When would they review/monitor; at what time intervals?

◆   What approaches would they take – using a committee meeting, a separate review day, with all the group members, with a sub group?

◆   How would they celebrate achievements and success?

◆   How would they help the group re-plan?

The action reflection cycle

Community development work has at its centre the concept that community groups and workers learn through reflection on practice. The action reflection cycle is one way of putting this principle into practice. In essence the model says that once a group has had an experience it needs to reflect upon it, look at what worked and what didn't, and then to think about what it would do differently next time.

The action reflection cycle

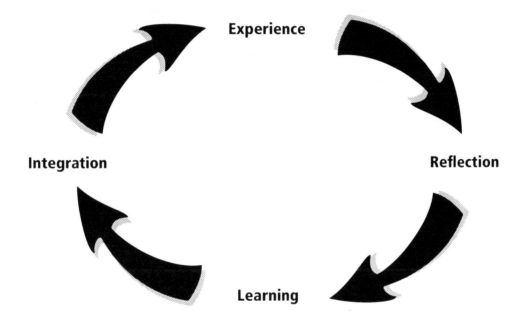

Experience

Reflection

Learning

Integration

When you are starting a new group it is good practice to build in reflection right from the start. For example the group might have run a visioning session (the experience), and afterwards it needs to sit down and talk about:

◆ How did it go? Who came? Who didn't? Did it achieve what we wanted it to? What worked? What didn't go so well? *(Reflection)*

◆ What can we learn from this event? What could we do differently next time? What would we keep the same? *(Learning)*

◆ When planning the next event the group looks at its notes and puts its reflection into practice *(Integration)*

◆ It then holds its next event and has another experience and the cycle starts again.

Reflective Journal

To be completed after each 4 hours of group work

Name of participant _____

Name of Tutor/s _____

1 Give a brief description of the topics covered by the group work and highlight your main areas of learning.

2 What did you think and feel about the group? What did you contribute to the group and its work?

3 Did you find anything difficult in the session and/or are there areas you would like us to cover again?

Portfolio question

You need to demonstrate an understanding of the processes involved when a group or network sets its objectives and priorities.

For level 2 You should describe two participatory techniques for involving members in setting the groups aims and objectives.

NB: the evidence for this will be collected in the next session.

For level 3 You should:

1. Analyse, by giving examples, different methods available to groups and networks to establish their aims and objectives

2. Explain your role in assisting a group or a network to agree its purpose and structure.

NB: the evidence for this will be collected in the next session.

(Complete during the week)

Make notes of anything or thoughts that have occurred during the week which you feel challenged you, or re-emphasised your beliefs/experiences.

Tutor's comments

Signature of participant _____

Signature of tutor/s _____ Date _____

How groups organise effectively

How groups organise effectively
Session Plan 7 and 8

◆ **Target audience**

People involved in and working with community groups

◆ **Length of session**

2 x 2-hour sessions; four hours in total

◆ **Session aim(s)**

● To explore how groups can organise effectively

◆ **Session outcomes**

At the end of the session students/trainees will…

● Appreciate the different ways or organising collectively

● Demonstrate an understanding of what makes for an effective group or network

◆ **Indicative content**

● Roles people take in groups

● People changing roles; getting stuck in roles

● Using people's skills in a group

● Decision-making in a group

● Communication and barriers to communication within groups

● Assertiveness and other types of behaviour

● Understanding change and how to handle it

● How to organise effectively as a group

● Rights and responsibilities

● Effects of structures on power relationships within groups.

Detailed Session Plan 7

Time	Content	Exercise/Method	Resources	Notes core topic or optional if time
0.00	Warm up			
0.10	Reflective journals; aims of day	Collect in journals. Tutor input on aims of day		
0.15	Tasks and roles that have to be undertaken within a group – formal and informal	Tutor input and small groups to explore roles taken within groups	Tutor Prompt Sheet 22	
0.45	Ways to organise to ensure tasks/roles covered	Scenarios of different types of groups	Tutor Prompt Sheet 23 Worksheet 7 with scenarios	
1.30	Handling change – to roles and people	Tutor input Paired role play	Tutor Prompt Sheet 24 with role play scenarios	
2.00	End			

Roles in groups

There are different roles that people in groups need to take in order for the group to function effectively. These can be formal and informal roles, some are task-focused roles, others are more about the process and maintenance of the group itself.

Split the group into four and give each a flip chart with one of the following headings. Ask them to think of all the roles relating to that heading.

1.   **Formal roles**

2.   **Task orientated roles**

3.   **Social/maintenance roles**

4.   **Individualistic roles (usually destructive for the group).**

The kinds of answers you would expect back for these include:

1   **Formal roles:** the positions that people get elected to or volunteered for in most groups; chair, secretary, treasurer, press officer, event organiser, etc.

Researchers Benne and Sheats identified several roles which relate to the completion of the group's task.

2   **Task roles:**

◆   Initiator-contributor: generates new ideas

◆   Information-seeker: asks for information about the task

◆   Questioner: asks lots of questions about what the group is doing and why

◆   Opinion-seeker: asks for the input from the group about its values

◆   Information-giver: offers facts or generalisations to the group

◆   Opinion-giver: states their beliefs about a group issue

◆   Elaborator-clarifier: explains ideas within the group, offers examples to clarify ideas

◆   Co-ordinator: shows the relationships between ideas

◆   Orienter: shifts the direction of the group's discussion

◆   Evaluator-critic: measures group's actions against some objective standard

◆   Energiser: stimulates the group to a higher level of activity

◆   Procedural-technician: performs logistical functions for the group

◆   Recorder: keeps a record of group actions.

---

3 **Social/maintenance roles:**

◆ Encourager-supporter: praises the ideas of others and encourages them

◆ Sharer: brings a more personal angle to what the group is doing, helps people relate informally and develop relationships

◆ Joker: provides light relief and an opportunity for the group to let off steam

◆ Harmoniser: mediates differences between group members

◆ Compromiser: moves group to another position that is favoured by all group members

◆ Gatekeeper/expediter: keeps communication channels open

◆ Standard setter: suggests standards or criteria for the group to achieve

◆ Group observer: keeps records of group activities and uses this information to offer feedback to the group

◆ Follower: goes along with the group and accepts the group's ideas.

---

4 **Individualistic roles:** These roles place the individual group member above the group itself and are destructive to the group:

◆ Aggressor: attacks other group members, deflates the status of others, and other aggressive behaviour

◆ Blocker: resists movement by the group

◆ Recognition seeker: calls attention to himself or herself

◆ Self-confessor: seeks to disclose non-group related feelings or opinions

◆ Dominator: asserts control over the group by manipulating the other group members

◆ Help seeker: tries to gain the sympathy of the group

◆ Special interest pleader: uses stereotypes to assert his or her own prejudices.

Ask the groups to feedback in turn and allow other groups to add anything they can.

Organising effectively

Worksheet 7 and the scenarios overleaf are designed to get people to think about different ways to organise to meet different objectives. In small groups, give participants a scenario, or create your own

Introduce the subject by recapping on the last sessions and by giving some examples of how different structures suit different types of groups. Here are a couple of examples in case you do not have local ones that are relevant:

◆ A campaigning group needs to be very flexible, able to respond quickly, use the media effectively, mobilise people quickly, hassle the councillors

◆ A group running services under a service level agreement/contract need to be able to ensure consistency and quality and so will need to allocate tasks to people who can follow them through, it will need to ensure limited liability for its committee members, it will need to be able to gather information to show it is doing what it said it would, it will need good negotiators and effective financial system.

The worksheet asks the groups to think about how the scenario group should organise itself. This means thinking about how it will meet, where, when, what methods of communication it will use, what structure it wants – one group, working groups, independent cells, etc.

Then it asks them to think about the formal roles required by this structure, followed by the informal roles.

The last question is about how they can find out what skills, knowledge and expertise the group members have amongst themselves. You may need to give some input about ways that groups can do their own audits. Here are some examples:

◆ Produce a bingo sheet with the skills, etc., needed and ask people to go round the group and find out who can do what

◆ Ask members of the group to interview each other

◆ Produce a list of what is needed and ask people to tick what they can offer.

This should build on one of the exercises from Session 5.

Scenarios

1 The local authority has transferred all its housing to a not-for-profit company run by a housing association. The housing association wants the tenants to develop an advisory group which can act as a bridge between the tenants and the association. It wants the advisory group to raise issues and problems expressed by tenants and to pass back information to the tenants from the association.

2 A group has formed to oppose the local school's application for outline planning permission for housing to be built on its playing fields. The school wants to sell the land to build new sports facilities. This is the fourth attempt by the school to sell the land.

3 The local authority is divesting itself of all its buildings and has offered a community association the building it has been meeting in for some time. It is offered to the community association to run as a not-for-profit business and to take over all the lettings as well as the maintenance.

4 A local environmental action team has been formed as an umbrella group to co-ordinate all the environmental projects in the city – from the city farm, to the Friends of the local woods, the schools environmental projects, and so forth. The umbrella group will ensure that resources are attracted and used well, and that there is less duplication and competition amongst groups working on environmental issues.

Ways to organise effectively

You have been given a scenario of a particular type of group. Read it through together and get a shared picture of the group. Then answer these questions.

1 **How could it best organise itself? Does it need to meet? How often? Can it work on telephone/email contacts? Should it have working groups?**

2 **What formal roles does this group need?**

3 **What other roles will it need?**

4 **How could it find out what skills, knowledge, expertise its members have?**

People changing roles

People changing, or wanting to change roles but not being allowed to, is a feature of the voluntary and community sector. Often someone starts off in a group with one role and gets stuck with it for ever until they leave. This can be an informal role – like the joker who only joked on the first meeting because they were nervous but is expected to be the joker for ever more. Or it can be formal – like a treasurer who can't find anyone to taken over from them. A founder or key member of a committee may decide they want the paid job when the organisation gets funding and find the transition from being a management committee member to being a staff member difficult to make.

Refer back to the earlier sessions on conflict and change and the exercises on understanding how we react to change – some people thriving on it and others hating it.

If community development is to fulfil its potential of enabling people to grow and to learn from each other, community development workers need to find ways to help people to move on and to be able to feel confident and skilled enough to take on new roles.

Put people into pairs and ask them to decide who will be the community development worker and who will be the group member. Give them a scenario and ask them to role play this and find a solution. They will share their ideas with the rest of the group during feedback.

Role Play scenarios

1 You are the treasurer of an advice centre and you have been doing this for some time now. The centre has just got money for some paid staff and you dread having to take on the payroll work as well as everything else as you don't have the time or the skills. You wish you could get the group to find a new treasurer who knows how to do this kind of work although you will miss being involved.

You are the community development worker; you know that the treasurer is feeling stressed and unsure about how to cope with the expansion of the centre. You have some ideas about the local development agencies such as the CVS/Voluntary Action taking on the payroll as the advice centre has enough money to pay for this. You also know about some training courses for treasurers. You have thought about setting up a finance sub committee to support the treasurer.

2 You are the newly appointed project manager, but you used to be chair of the organisation until it was recently given some money. The committee has held an away day to look at how it can manage the organisation. They started to question some of the actions you have taken. They are starting to ask for you to let them know in advance before you commit the organisation to new areas of work, and you resent this.

You are a community development worker who is on the management committee of this project. During the away day you noticed that the project manager was beginning to block and withdraw as the committee started to get itself organised. The committee want to re-assure the project manager that they trust her. They also want to help her let go of her previous role as chair and to help her move into the manager's job properly, working with the committee.

---

3 You have recently joined a group which aims to collect together the history of the area and make people more aware of its past. Your background is in organising a trade union and you like to get things done. You think this group is being very slow and is too involved in thinking things through in detail. The group worries about the right ways to do things, like who should interview who, and how should the interviews be recorded. You are getting frustrated because its taking a long time to get nowhere as far as you can see.

You are a community development worker who has supported a group of local people to get a small heritage lottery grant to research and record the history of the local area. They are committed to spending time working out the best way to involve people and to collect lots of different stories. They are aware of the need to proceed carefully and slowly otherwise people in the community may get put off and not be prepared to be recorded. The people in the group need to gain confidence in preparing for the interviews and in using the recording equipment. You think that the group approach is the right one given the communities in the area, and you also think that the new person has a lot to offer if only they could begin to see that the process was as important as the task in such a group.

Detailed Session Plan 8

Time	Content	Exercise/Method	Resources	Notes *core topic or optional if time*
0.00	Wake up			
0.10	Communications within groups. What is needed and why it doesn't happen automatically	Buzz groups – ideas for where communication takes place within groups. Tutor story of miscommunications. Barriers to communication and small group work	Tutor Prompt Sheet 25	
0.40	Different types of behaviour – aggressive, assertive, manipulative etc	Tutor input on different kinds of behaviour. Role plays	Tutor Prompt Sheet 26 Handout 11	
1.10	Decision-making processes	Exercise on getting the steps right. Different types of decision-making and their impact on the group	Tutor Prompt Sheet 27 Exercise on decision making Handout 12 Worksheet 8	
1.45	Reflective journals		Reflective journal 4	
1.50	Ending game			
2.00	End			

Group Work Skills • **Session Eight**
Federation for Community Development Learning

Communications within groups

Part ❶

Ask people to turn to the person next to them (buzz groups) and come up with some ideas of where communication takes place within groups. You can give some examples to get them going, such as a member reporting back from a meeting with another group; correspondence received; debates on policy, and so on.

Collect all the ideas and record them on a flip chart.

Part ❷

Tell a story about the family who were together one hot sunny afternoon. They had finished lunch and were sitting around when one person said, 'Why don't we go out, we could drive to the shop in the next county which makes its own ice cream'. Another one agreed and said; 'Okay I'll get the car keys'. So they all went out and drove through the heat for a couple of hours, getting stuck in various traffic jams on the way. They found the place, bought their ice creams, ate them and then drove home which took another two hours and lots more sitting in traffic jams. When they got back, one person said, 'Well that was nice' but the driver said; 'I don't think so, why did we go all that way in the heat to buy an ice cream, I would rather have stayed here'. But said the first person; 'I thought you wanted to go'. 'No' was the reply, 'I just went along with the idea as you all seemed to want to go'. They all looked at the person who had made the suggestion in the beginning and said; 'Well I didn't want to go either, I was just trying to think up ideas about what we could do and you seemed keen to go with the first one I made…' And it turned out that no-one really wanted to go.

This gives an example of how miscommunication can happen very easily. Ask group members to think of times when they thought that communications had become distorted in their groups.

Part ❸

Make a list of some of the common problems around communication.

Split the group into smaller groups and give them a number of the problems/barriers around communication and ask them to come up with ideas for avoiding or tackling these problems. These can be structural suggestions, or personal development ideas.

Let each group feedback and open up each point for discussion.

Types of behaviour

Give out Handout 11 and explain the different kinds of behaviour.

Split the participants in four small groups and give each one of them a type of behaviour:

◆ Aggressive

◆ Passive

◆ Manipulative

◆ Assertive.

Give each group the same scenario and ask them to act it out using their behaviour type.

A suitable scenario could be:

A few people in a group have just found out that the chair had decided to hold a Christmas party in a pub run by his brother-in-law and that a full roast meal would be served. He has committed the group to paying for this but has not discussed it with anyone. Within the group there would be vegetarians, non-drinkers, non-Christians.

Ask each group to think about how to portray their type of behaviour and to act it out – the rest of the group have to guess what type of behaviour is being displayed.

Different types of behaviour

Aggressive	Goes all out to win, attacks others, belittles and puts down; is often pushy, goes too far, forces themselves on others, allows no room for others' choices, can be cruel, offensive and rude; domineering, taking over, a 'last word' person; argumentative; arrogant; overreacting
Passive	Sometimes known as non-assertive; opts out, moans a lot, puts themselves down, plays at being helpless; martyr syndrome, suffers in silences, feels unappreciated; wanting to be liked; apologetic
Manipulative	Indirect, devious, dropping hints, sulking, punishing others, sarcastic; controlling, making others feel guilty; going round the houses to ask for something, denies feelings
Assertive	Direct, honest, respects others, sincere; responsible for what they want, their thoughts and actions; independent of others approval; respecting difference; confronting fears; sense of self worth and self esteem; able to express their needs, preferences and feelings.

In any group there may be people exhibiting all these kinds of behaviours. The first three can all lead to miscommunications and misunderstandings. The aim should be to develop assertive behaviour as the norm within the group so that the group members can communicate in a direct, honest way which respects each other and takes responsibility for themselves.

Assertive behaviour is characterised by being:

◆ Clear – stating clearly what is needed, what you want to say/do/ask for/feel

◆ Honest – being prepared to state your thoughts, feelings, ideas, opinions as you see or feel them, not necessarily as you think others want to hear them

◆ Direct – coming to the point quickly – not 'beating about the bush' which can lead to people being confused about what you are saying

◆ Appropriate – it fits the situation and does not attempt to divert or deflect discussions with irrelevant points

◆ Respectful – of yourself and others; recognising differences and being prepared for negotiation and compromise; asking questions and listening

◆ Personal – speaking for yourself, using 'I' statements; speaking to a person, rather than about them.

Decision-making

Organise the participants into smaller groups. Give out the exercise sheet; along with cut up slips of the 7 steps and the actions and ask them to put them into the right order.

In the whole group ask them to think about the different types of decision-making they know about:

◆   Does it involve everyone in the group or are some decisions made by just a few people?

◆   Does the group try and reach consensus or do people vote?

◆   Do some people have more formal weight than others, for example, chair's casting vote?

Make a list of the types of decision-making systems that people know about.

Give out Handout 12 and Worksheet 8. Ask them to decide appropriate decision-making processes.

The seven steps

Define the problem

Prioritise

Generate alternatives

Evaluate alternatives

Decide

Implement

Evaluate

Actions involved

Diagnose the nature and the causes	Evaluate acceptability
Categorise the problems	Evaluate costs
Search for any changing circumstances	Evaluate risks
	Evaluate reversibility
Analyse criteria for successful solution	Check for support/dissent
Specify objectives	Select the agreed alternative
Decide when to tackle the problem	Decide who should implement
Agree who should make the decision	Draw up a plan and timetable for implementation
	Implement decision
Brainstorm ideas	Communicate decision
Consult with others for ideas	Record and evaluate the process
Evaluate feasibility	Plan when to evaluate the effectiveness of the decision over time

Group Work Skills • **Session Eight**
Federation for Community Development Learning

Exercise on decision-making

There are 7 steps in good decision-making; arrange the steps in order and then put the actions along side them.

Steps	Actions involved
1	
2	
3	
4	
5	
6	
7	

The decision making process

When you are involved in making a group decision, using the process outlined below can assist you in reaching good decisions.

Step	Action
Define the Problem	Diagnose the nature and the causes Categorise the problems Search for any changing circumstances Analyse criteria for successful solution Specify objectives.
Prioritise	Decide when to tackle the problem Agree who should make the decision.
Generate Alternatives	Brainstorm ideas Consult with others for ideas.
Evaluate Alternatives	Evaluate feasibility Evaluate acceptability. Evaluate costs Evaluate risks Evaluate reversibility.
Decide	Check for support/dissent Select the agreed alternative Decide who should implement Draw up a plan and timetable for implementation.
Implement	Implement decision Communicate decision.
Evaluate	Record and evaluate the process Plan when to evaluate the effectiveness of the decision over time.

Appropriate decision making

In your group decide on the appropriate decision-making system for the following groups/networks

A network of Disabled people who 'meet' using the internet and who are aiming to set up a web-based information centre for Disabled people	
A campaigning group formed to save the local school from being closed down and the pupils being sent to another one a couple of miles away	
A support group for carers of people with long-term mental health difficulties	
A lottery funded after-school group which employs part-time tutors	

Reflective Journal

To be completed after each 4 hours of group work

Name of participant _____

Name of Tutor/s _____

1 Give a brief description of the topics covered by the group work and highlight your main areas of learning.

2 What did you think and feel about the group? What did you contribute to the group and its work?

3 Did you find anything difficult in the session and/or are there areas you would like us to cover again?

Portfolio question

You need to demonstrate an appreciation of the different ways of organising collectively and demonstrate an understanding of what makes for an effective group/network.

For level 2 You should:

1. Identify two issues of communication that can arise in groups/networks and suggest ways to improve communication

2. Identify the range of roles that need to be taken in a group/network

3. Explain how people's skills can be used effectively within a group/network

4. Suggest two ways to support and encourage active participation by group or network members.

For level 3 You should:

1. Identify communication blocks that need to be negotiated and resolved

2. Analyse the different roles taken within a group/network, and explain why they are important

3. Describe, with examples, different ways that groups/networks can organise to meet their aims and objectives.

(Complete during the week)

Make notes of anything or thoughts that have occurred during the week which you feel challenged you, or re-emphasised your beliefs/experiences.

Tutor's comments

Signature of participant _____

Signature of tutor/s _____ Date _____

Developing inclusive groups

Developing inclusive groups
Session Plan 9 and 10

◆ **Target audience**

People involved in and working with community groups

◆ **Length of session**

2 x 2-hour sessions; four hours in total

◆ **Session aim(s)**

● To explore ways to develop inclusive groups that grow and learn together

◆ **Session outcomes**

At the end of the session students/trainees will…

● Demonstrate an understanding of the issues of inclusion and exclusion within groups or networks

◆ **Indicative content**

● Team working

● Promoting participation and involvement of all group members

● Developing the skills of people in a group

● Diversity within groups to reflect the wider community

● Bringing people to create more inclusive groups

● Awareness of others – needs, rights, responsibilities

● Publicity

● Encouraging reflection in the group

● Creating opportunities for shared learning and development

● Different approaches to tackling oppressive practices

● ADP group work.

Detailed Session Plan 9

Time	Content	Exercise/Method	Resources	Notes *core topic or optional if time*
0.00	Warm up			
0.10	Reflective journals; aims of day	Collect in any journals. Tutor input on aim of session	Session plan	
0.15	What do we mean by a team/ team working?	Pairs to consider the key words that spring to mind when thinking of a team. Different ideas about what a team is. What roles are needed in a team?	Tutor Prompt Sheet 28 Handouts 13 and 14	
0.40	How to ensure participation/ involvement of all group members	Scenario of a team review day	Tutor Prompt Sheet 29 Exercise sheet on a review day	
1.10	Developing the skills and knowledge of group members through sharing of experiences and creating opportunities for working with others	Different ways to skill up people – worksheet	Tutor Prompt Sheet 30 Worksheet 9	
1.30	Bringing in new people to ensure it reflects the wider community	Responding to changes in the local population; case study	Tutor Prompt Sheet 31	
2.00	End			

What is a team?

The aim of this exercise is to get people to think about what they understand by the word team and to appreciate that different people have different ideas as to what makes a team. This can sometimes lead to conflict when expectations are not met, for example over the level of commitment expected to be given to a team by its' members.

The first part of this exercise is to put group members into pairs and ask them to write down the main words that spring to mind when they are asked to 'define a team'. Ask them to put each word or phrase on a separate post-it note.

Collect the post-it notes in by asking someone to give one word or phrase and then ask if other pairs have anything similar – group them together on a flip chart. Work through the key words and phrases until all of them have been used.

The second part of the exercise requires you to hold a group discussion on the differences that have come up. These might include different ideas about how close or tight-knit a team should be, how much attachment people might have to a team – some might want to belong just to achieve a task, others to gain support and friendship. Ask for examples of where there has been different expectations about what a team should be like and the tensions that this can cause.

The third part is about the roles that people take in team; there are two handouts and you can choose which to use depending on the interests of participants.

◆   Handout 13 is a version of the Belbin Team Roles – there is a summary sheet and the full scale questionnaire if you want to use it.

◆   Handout 14 is about four different team types.

Either of these approaches should lead into a discussion about the different roles needed within a team.

Team roles

BELBIN Team-Role Type	Contributions	Characteristic behaviour	Allowable Weaknesses
PLANT	Creative, imaginative, unorthodox. Solves difficult problems. Brings vision and stimulation	Good at ideas, poor at follow through; radical approach to problems; responds to the co-ordinator, ignores other team members	Ignores details. Too pre-occupied to communicate effectively. Wants to spend team time on their ideas; poor at taking criticism
CO-ORDINATOR	Mature, confident, a good chairperson. Clarifies goals, promotes decision-making, delegates well	Focuses people on what they do best; brings out the best in others; assertive but not domineering; good communicator; motivates others	Can often be seen as manipulative. Off loads personal work. Not brilliant or outstandingly creative
MONITOR EVALUATOR	Sober, strategic and discerning. Sees all options. Judges accurately	Assimilates and evaluates large quantities of information; mulls things over; objective approach to problems; finds faults on others	Lacks drive and ability to inspire others. Unexciting. Can lower morale
IMPLEMENTER	Disciplined, reliable, conservative and efficient. Turns ideas into practical actions	Methodical and systematic; responsible and hard working; doesn't like airy fairy ideas; always knows what's going on	Somewhat inflexible. Slow to respond to new possibilities. Can be thrown by sudden changes. Status conscious

COMPLETER FINISHER	Painstaking, conscientious, anxious. Searches out errors and omissions. Delivers on time	Compulsive about deadlines and order; needs to check all the detail personally; impatient with other team members	Inclined to worry unduly. Reluctant to delegate
RESOURCE INVESTIGATOR	Extrovert, enthusiastic, communicative. Explores opportunities. Develops contacts	Know someone who can help out; rarely in the office; positive and enthusiastic, relaxed and sociable; active under pressure; good improviser	Over-optimistic. Loses interest once initial enthusiasm has passed; easily bored, demoralised and ineffective
SHAPER	Challenging, dynamic, thrives on pressure. The drive and courage to overcome obstacles. Pushes team to make decisions	Driving; competitive; quick to challenge and to respond to challenges; often rows but doesn't hold grudges; exudes self-confidence; only reassured by results	Prone to provocation. Offends people's feelings. Can be abrasive and arrogant. Impulsive, impatient and easily frustrated
TEAMWORKER	Co-operative, mild, perceptive and diplomatic. Listens, builds, averts friction	Listener, bringing people into discussions, counselling team members, organises social events	Indecisive in crunch situations. Avoids confrontation

More details on www.belbin.com/meridith

Team roles for teamwork

This article is based on training sources in common usage. It draws on the work of Meredith Belbin and its subsequent development.

Team roles questionnaire

Task:

For each section distribute a total of 10 points among the sentences according to how you would describe your behaviour. Within each section you may allocate the 10 points in any way, providing the score for (a) to (h) adds up to 10. You may transfer your score directly on to the score sheet provided.

Section ① What I believe I can contribute to a team

(a) I think I can quickly see and take advantage of opportunities.

(b) I can work well with a wide range of people.

(c) Producing ideas is one of my natural assets.

(d) My ability rests in being able to draw people out whenever I detect they have something of value to contribute to group objectives.

(e) My capacity to follow through has much to do with my personal effectiveness.

(f) I am ready to face temporary unpopularity if it leads to worthwhile results in the end.

(g) I am quick to sense what is likely to work in a situation with which I am familiar.

(h) I can offer a reasoned case for alternative courses of action without introducing bias or prejudice.

Section ② If I have a possible shortcoming in teamwork, it could be that:

(a) I am not at ease unless meetings are well structured and controlled and generally well conducted.

(b) I am inclined to be too generous towards others who have a valid viewpoint that has not been given a proper airing.

(c) I have a tendency to talk a lot once the group gets on to new ideas.

(d) My objective outlook makes it difficult for me to join in readily and enthusiastically with colleagues.

(e) I am sometimes seen as forceful and authoritarian if there is a need to get something done.

(f) I find it difficult to lead from the front, perhaps because I am over-responsive to group atmosphere.

(g) I am apt to get too caught up in ideas that occur to me and so lose track of what is happening.

(h) My colleagues tend to see me as worrying unnecessarily over detail and the possibility that things may go wrong.

Section ❸ When involved in a project with other people:

(a) I have an aptitude for influencing people without pressuring them.

(b) My general vigilance prevents careless mistakes and omissions being made.

(c) I am ready to press for action to make sure that the meeting doesn't waste time or lose sight of the main objective.

(d) I can be counted upon to contribute something original.

(e) I am always ready to back a good suggestion in the common interest.

(f) I am keen to look for the latest in new ideas and developments.

(g) I believe my capacity for cool judgement is appreciated by others.

(h) I can be relied upon to see all essential work is organised.

Section ❹ My characteristic approach to group work is:

(a) I have a quiet interest in getting to know colleagues better.

(b) I am not reluctant to challenge the views of others or to hold a minority view myself.

(c) I can usually find a line of argument to refute unsound propositions.

(d) I think I have a talent for making things work once a plan is put into operation.

(e) I have a tendency to avoid the obvious and to come out with the unexpected.

(f) I bring a touch of perfectionism to any team job I undertake.

(g) I am ready to make use of contacts outside the group itself.

(h) While I am interested in all views, I have no hesitation in making up my mind once a decision has to be made.

Section ❺ I gain satisfaction in a job because:

(a) I enjoy analysing situations and weighing up all the possible choices.

(b) I am interested in finding practical solutions to problems.

(c) I like to feel I am fostering good working relationships.

(d) I can have a strong influence on decisions.

(e) I can meet people who may have something new to offer.

(f) I can get people to agree on a necessary course of action.

(g) I feel in my element where I can give a task my full attention.

(h) I like to find a field that stretches my imagination.

Section 6 If I am suddenly given a difficult task with limited resources and unfamiliar people:

(a) I would feel like retiring to a corner to devise a way out of the impasse before developing a line.

(b) I would be ready to work with the person who showed the most positive approach, however difficult he or she might be.

(c) I would find some way of reducing the size of the task by establishing what different individuals might best contribute.

(d) My natural sense of urgency would help to ensure that we did not fall behind schedule,

(e) I believe I would keep cool and maintain my capacity to think straight.

(f) I would retain a steadiness of purpose in spite of the pressures.

(g) I would be prepared to take a positive lead if I felt the group was making no progress.

(h) I would open up discussions with a view to stimulating new thoughts and getting something moving.

Section 7 With reference to the problems to which I am subject in working groups:

(a) I am apt to show my impatience with those who are obstructing progress.

(b) Others might criticise me for being too analytical and insufficiently intuitive.

(c) My desire to ensure that work is properly done can hold up proceedings.

(d) I tend to get bored rather easily and rely on one or two stimulating members to spark me off.

(e) I find it difficult to get started unless the goals are clear.

(f) I am sometimes poor at explaining and clarifying complex points that occur to me.

(g) I am conscious of demanding from others the things I cannot do myself.

(h) I hesitate to get my points across when I run up against real opposition.

Team roles questionnaire: scoring sheet

Task

1 Transfer scores from each section on to the first grid.

For example, if in Section 1 you allocated 6 points to (a) then you write 6 under 'a' opposite 1.

Grid 1 Section	a	b	c	d	e	f	g	h
1								
2								
3								
4								
5								
6								
7								
Totals								

2 Then transfer scores from grid 1 on to grid 2.

Your score of 6 under 'a' in grid 1 is entered in box 'a' of grid 2.

Grid 2	CH	SH	PL	RI	CW	TW	ME	CF
1	d=	f=	c=	a=	g=	b=	h=	e=
2	b=	e=	g=	c=	a=	f=	d=	h=
3	a=	c=	d=	f=	h=	e=	g=	b=
4	h=	b=	e=	g=	d=	a=	c=	f=
5	f=	d=	h=	e=	b=	c=	a=	g=
6	c=	g=	a=	h=	f=	b=	e=	d=
7	g=	a=	f=	d=	e=	h=	b=	c=
Totals								

3 Total scores – your highest score indiicates your primary role

Key			
CH Chairperson	**ME** Monitor Evaluator	**SH** Shaper
TW Teamworker	**RI** Resource Investigator	**CF** Completer/Finisher
PL Plant	**CW** Company worker	

Team types

These four types each represent different aspects of how people may operate in group settings. The basic four categories have emerged out of many different cultures. Models like it show up in many indigenous traditions (Celtic Wheel of Being, Native American Medicine Wheel, and so on), modern science's analysis of the human brain and team theory.

The four different types are designated by the four directions (and in most indigenous traditions have some associated items or animals; below includes the Lakota Medicine Wheel's and the Celtic Wheel of Being's objects or animals)

East

(eagle, visionary/explorer, yellow, spring, creative, inventive, has fire of inspiration)

◆ Sees the big picture

◆ Very idea-oriented, focuses on future thought

◆ Insight into mission and purpose

◆ Likes to experiment and explore

◆ Can lose focus on tasks and not follow through

◆ May become easily overwhelmed, lose track of time

◆ Tends to be highly enthusiastic early on then burns out.

South

(mouse, producer, green, summer, hearth fire, fertility, bringing together)

◆ Allows others to feel important in determining direction of what's happening

◆ Value-driven regarding all aspects of personal/professional life

◆ Uses relationships to accomplish tasks

◆ Innocence and trust in others based on vulnerability and openness

◆ Supportive, nurturing, feeling based

◆ Has trouble saying 'no' to requests

◆ Internalises difficulty and assumes blame

◆ Prone to disappointment when relationship is seen as secondary to task

◆ Difficulty confronting, dealing with anger.

West

(bear, judge, brown, autumn, learning, judgement, information)

◆ Weighs all sides of issues

◆ Uses data analysis and logic

◆ Seen as practical and thorough in task situations

◆ Introspective, self-analytical

◆ Can become stubborn and entrenched in position

◆ Can be indecisive, collect unnecessary data, mired in details

◆ May appear cold, withdrawn.

North

(buffalo, white, winter, warrior, open to struggle, decisive)

◆ Assertive, active, decisive

◆ Like to be in control of relationship and steer course of events

◆ Quick to act, expresses sense of urgency for others to act now

◆ Enjoys challenge of difficult situations and people

◆ Can get defensive quickly, argue, try to out-expert you

◆ Can lose patience, pushes for decision before it's time

◆ May get autocratic, want things their way, ride roughshod over people.

Ensuring participation by all team members

The group will be asked to work in smaller groups to design a team review and planning day (exercise sheet on organising a team review day).

In order to prepare them for this ask them to think about the principles/ground-rules which should underlay a team review day, for example:

◆ That everyone has the right to contribute

◆ That different methods need to be used to get the best out of people

◆ That it should be clear about its aims

◆ That people's different experiences should be valued.

Write all their ideas on a flip chart and leave them displayed on a nearby wall.

Ask the group if they have come across any participatory exercises which could be used on a review and planning day. You might want to suggest some techniques such as:

◆ Pictures of bricks on A4 paper where people can write on the foundations that they think the team can build on

◆ Bricks can also be used to build a wall of problems which need to be taken down

◆ Different coloured large or small jigsaw shapes which people can use to write on what they have in place and what gaps need filling

◆ Flame shapes to show what motivates and inspires, water drops to show what dampens down people's enthusiasm

◆ Storytelling technique of a group creating their own story about what they would like the group to be by each person adding in another sentence

◆ A large group drawing of everyone's ideas about what the group could be like/do

◆ Each person has an individual sheet with a stick person in the middle and around it people write what skills, knowledge, experience they bring with them to the team.

Once people have got the idea of different participatory ways of engaging people to create a fun but purposeful day, give out the exercise sheet overleaf and ask them to plan this day and to decide what methods would be suitable.

Allow time for feedback on the different ideas and discussion.

Organising a team review day

You are a member of a team of community development workers for an area. You are managed by a local management committee made up of local residents, representatives of local projects and with advisors from the local council. The team was set up with three-year funding from trusts and the lottery. All the team are now in post and some new people have joined the management committee.

The suggestion is made for all of the team and the management committee to spend a day together to review progress so far and to plan ahead for the future of the project. The hope is that this will lead to a greater involvement by the new committee members, and that the best use can be made of the skills and expertise of all the team and committee.

You have been asked to draw up plans for this event which will ensure that everyone participates and that a clear action plan is drawn up by the end of it which identifies who will be doing what within the project. Note down the ideas that you have for this day.

Ways that people can help each other to learn

In this exercise you are encouraging people to think about all the ways that people can help each other to learn through sharing their experiences and expertise.

Give out Worksheet 9 and explain what each of these types of learning involves and give some examples. For example shadowing can be used to help a person learn about book-keeping. Action learning sets are made up of people with a similar job who get together to explore common issues, such as project managers in an area.

The worksheet doesn't have training courses as an option although the participants may choose to add in running in-house courses or providing training courses open to others. The reasoning is to try and get people to think more widely about different ways that learning opportunities can be created.

Ask people to work in groups of three to complete the worksheet, and organise feedback to get all the ideas on one approach before moving onto the next one.

Learning from others

In your team of workers and management committee members you have people with very different skills, knowledge and experience. Your project only has a limited training budget.

Below are some different ways that people can be helped to develop their skills and knowledge by learning from others. For each of the different approaches think of examples of what type of skill, experience, knowledge this method would be suitable for.

Method of learning	Suitable for
Visits to other project	
Mentoring	
Shadowing	
Buddying	
Apprenticeship	
Action learning sets	
Working groups	
Job or task sharing	
Your other ideas	

Bringing in new people

This exercise is designed to get participants to think about how a group responds to changes in the population make up of their community.

Give an example of a fairly well established group who have a fairly broad brief, such as health, play, young people, community safety or something similar. Choose one or more examples that most of the participants can relate to.

Explain that when the group was set up it tried hard to make sure that all the different groupings within the community were invited to become involved. Over the past couple of years there have been a number of changes to the make up of the community, which the group needs to respond to.

Examples of changes could include:

◆ The settlement of a number of refugee and asylum seeking people

◆ The building of new flats for 'key workers'

◆ The refurbishment of old houses into flats for vulnerable people, undertaken by a local housing association

◆ The increased number of Black families buying houses in a previously white area as the families choose to leave the inner city areas

◆ An increase in the number of young people around as the families who first settled in the area when it was built ten years ago see their children grow up into adolescents.

Choose a number of relevant changes and ask the small groups to decide how this established organisation could involve members of these newer communities in their activities and work.

Detailed Session Plan 10

Time	Content	Exercise/Method	Resources	Notes core topic or optional if time
0.00	Wake up			
0.10	Prejudice, discrimination and oppression	Experiences within the group of individual and group discrimination and how it left people feeling	Tutor Prompt Sheet 32 Handout 15	
0.30	Issues arising from a diverse group working together	Case study	Tutor Prompt Sheet 33 Case study	
1.00	How to tackle oppressive and discriminatory behaviour	Small groups to look at some of the issues arising from the two previous exercises	Tutor Prompt Sheet 34 Handout 16 and 17	
1.40	Reflective journals			
1.50	Ending game			
2.00	End			

Understanding the words

In this exercise the aim is to explore people's understanding of working to promote equality and value diversity within groups by understanding prejudice, discrimination and oppression and the different approaches and their impact.

Start with asking people if they have ever felt treated less than others, discriminated against or oppressed. Ask them to make a note of the incidents and be prepared to share briefly the key points and how it left them feeling – log these on a flip chart.

Introduce Handout 15 on prejudice, discrimination and oppression. Discuss the differences, relate this to the value base and practice principles of community development work.

For example

◆ **Social Justice** principle talks about *'challenging oppressive and discriminatory actions and attitudes'*

◆ **Self determination** principle talks about *'promoting the view that communities do not have the right to oppress other communities'*.

Ask people to go into groups of three to discuss one or more of the examples given by group members. Ask them to think about what might have been behind the situation.

Prejudice, discrimination and oppression

Prejudice

◆ Any preconceived opinions or feeling, either favourable or unfavourable. (praejudicium = before judgment)

◆ Holding on to an attitude despite contrary available evidence, information or experience

◆ An unfavourable opinion or feeling formed beforehand or without knowledge, thought or reason

◆ Unreasonable feelings, opinions or attitudes, especially of a hostile nature, directed against a racial, religious, national group, or a group of people who are identifiable and different from our own

◆ Negative personal perceptions that discriminate against individuals seen only in terms of being representative of such a group

◆ Personal attitudes towards other people, usually based on negative group stereotypes which are not inborn but learned as children from adults and reinforced by the media and peer group talk

◆ A partial rejection of a person on the basis of his or her real or supposed specifiable characteristics

◆ A tendency towards biased judgements: normally perceived in others rather than ourselves

◆ An inability to move beyond an initial response of seeing someone in terms of a projected generalised label in one's mind rather than as a person.

Discrimination

◆ Discrimination is a term that has legal status

◆ It refers to unfair treatment based on differentials accorded to race and/or gender and disability (as well as age, sexual orientation, etc.)

◆ Discrimination in employment, in education and in housing, have been tackled to some extent in the Sex Discrimination Act 1975 and in the Equal Pay Act 1970

◆ The Disability Discrimination Act tries to tackle discrimination faced by disabled people in some aspects of their lives

◆ New legislation aims to outlaw discrimination on religious grounds

◆ However, the limitations of the legislation have been apparent, excluding as they do whole groups of workers and whole areas of discrimination. The legislation against discrimination is small in scope around 'equality' in relation to the profound character of for example, racism, sexism or disablism

◆ Legislation against discrimination is fundamentally reformist in orientation, for it is concerned with prompting small-scale changes, rather than any fundamental restructuring of power relationships or social values. For example the emphasis on sex discrimination diverts attention from the real problem of women's second class status

Discrimination contd.

◆ It is important that community development workers understand both the legislative aspects concerning discrimination and the personal dynamics of discrimination. It is also important that they understand the limitations of an anti-discriminatory approach. There are some areas of prejudice which the law does not cover and in some instances the law itself can be quite oppressive

◆ Anti-discriminatory practice works to a model of challenging unfairness.

Oppression

◆ The word 'oppress' comes from the Latin for 'to press on, to press against'. It suggests force, being flattened, squashed out of shape

◆ Oppression is a complex term, which relates to structural differences in power as well as to the personal experience of oppressing or being oppressed

◆ It relates to race, gender, sexual orientation, age, religion, and disability as separate domains and as overlapping experiences

◆ In understanding oppression we have to find a way of seeing that keeps in focus both the uniqueness and specificity of, for example, the oppression of race, while also seeing the interconnectedness of all oppressions

◆ For example the oppression of women as

women is impossible to analyse in isolation from other factors such as race, sexuality or disability. To deal with one without even alluding to the other is to distort our commonalities as well as our differences

◆ We need to acknowledge the specificity of the oppression and avoid ranking them so that some are more important than others

◆ We should not attempt to deal with oppression from a purely theoretical base but to use our emotions to help us grapple with the source of our own and others oppression

◆ When we think about the term and when we try to work with it, we must consider its personal relevance; the structural and ideological aspects; its common features and the specifics of oppression

◆ Creating this understanding is crucial to community development work because community work values require us to develop a framework for understanding the elements of oppression and its repercussions; the abuse of power, inequality and social injustice, stereotyping, socially constructed hierarchies of value and thereby differing life choices and access to services, discrimination, and so on

◆ Anti-oppressive practice works with a model of empowerment and liberation and requires a fundamental re-thinking of values, institutions and relationships and is

Impact on groups

The aim of this exercise is to get participants to be more aware of the way that prejudice, discrimination and oppression can be around in community groups and networks and have an adverse impact on the way the group operates and how well it meets local needs.

Use the case study below or create one based on the area that you are training in.

An old mill building was being converted into flats, some were to be sold as luxury flats, others were to rented out by a housing association to local families and some would be rented to the university for students to live in. The developers have offered some space on the ground floor as a community space.

The area surrounding the mill has a mixed population and includes:

◆   A small but ageing Polish population who had settled here after the Second World War. They have their own centre which is getting really run down and needs a lot of repairs

◆   A larger and growing Kashmiri community, with many young people who were born here. Their parents and grandparents had come to work in the mills in the 1960s and 1970s. There are some very small premises where the different groups meet but they are not large enough for sports activities

◆   A small and growing Chinese student community – as the university has made close links with China and has offered places to many Chinese students able to study in the UK

◆   Single women with young children who live in the housing association property. They use the local park in the summer but there is very little play space in the area and the nurseries can only offer part time provision

◆   Mental health service users and survivors who have been provided with housing by a specialist housing association in the area; some of them attend a MIND group in the centre of town but would like more local provision where they could meet and undertake writing and drama classes

◆   The Older Lesbian Network meets in a backroom of a local pub, but this pub is closing. They are looking for somewhere else to meet in the area as it's convenient for many members to get there although they come from all over the town

What are the issues that might arise when trying to bring all these groups together to explore joint use of the new community space?

Some of the issues that you might expect to come back from the groups could include:

◆ Those communities who have been around for a while and with existing but poor provision expecting to have priority over those they perceive as newcomers to the area

◆ Prejudices about the different religions

◆ Discriminatory attitudes between different ethnic communities

◆ Attitudes towards people living in different kinds of accommodation

◆ Different needs of older people and children

◆ Whether the needs of girls and young women have been considered as well as the demands of young men for sports

◆ Attitudes towards students from other countries who have not had a traditional link with the area

◆ Attitudes towards people with mental health difficulties

◆ Attitudes towards Lesbian, Gay and Bi-sexual people

◆ Fears about who will get the flats and the impact this will have on access to local services such as GPs and schools

◆ Practical matters – such as

    ❖ When to meet, day and time

    ❖ Communication – translators; giving people space to say their thoughts

    ❖ Child care and dependent care

    ❖ Where to meet.

An old mill building was being converted into flats, some were to be sold as luxury flats, others were to rented out by a housing association to local families and some would be rented to the university for students to live in. The developers have offered some space on the ground floor as a community space.

The area surrounding the mill has a mixed population and includes:

◆ A small but ageing Polish population who had settled here after the Second World War. They have their own centre which is getting really run down and needs a lot of repairs

◆ A larger and growing Kashmiri community, with many young people who were born here. Their parents and grandparents had come to work in the mills in the 1960s and 1970s. There are some very small premises where the different groups meet but they are not large enough for sports activities

◆ A small and growing Chinese student community – as the university has made close links with China and has offered places to many Chinese students able to study in the UK

◆ Single women with young children who live in the housing association property. They use the local park in the summer but there is very little play space in the area and the nurseries can only offer part time provision

◆ Mental health service users and survivors who have been provided with housing by a specialist housing association in the area; some of them attend a MIND group in the centre of town but would like more local provision where they could meet and undertake writing and drama classes

◆ The Older Lesbian Network meets in a backroom of a local pub, but this pub is closing. They are looking for somewhere else to meet in the area as it's convenient for many members to get there although they come from all over the town.

What are the issues that might arise when you try to bring all these groups together to explore joint use of the new community space?

Using the case study you have been given, work through your response using the following prompts.

What did I hear/see?	
What do I think is behind this?	
What approach do I want to achieve?	
Do I respond now or later?	
What action shall I take?	
What are the likely consequences?	

Tackling oppressive and discriminatory behaviour

This exercise follows on from the previous one by picking up on some of the issues that have been brought up and looking at how to respond.

You can start by talking about the different approaches to equality outlined in Handout 16. Discuss with the group the idea that the way we tackle discrimination and oppression is affected by what we think we are trying to achieve. The handouts suggests four different approaches.

The next part of the exercise is to introduce an approach to tackling oppressive and discriminatory behaviour which follows a pattern of:

◆ Checking out what you have heard or seen

◆ Deciding what is behind the words or actions

  ❖ Is it based on misinformation (such as the numbers of people seeking asylum)?

  ❖ Is it the result of well-intentioned but ill-thought out behaviour (treating disabled people inappropriately – the 'does he take sugar' syndrome)?

  ❖ Is it designed to upset and offend (deliberate use of words or excluding behaviour such as turning their back on someone)?

◆ Deciding on the best approach

  ❖ Do you need to correct the information and present accurate facts and data?

  ❖ Do you need to explain why the behaviour is causing offence and distress?

  ❖ Do you need to stop the behaviour and deal with it later?

◆ What do you want to achieve?

  ❖ Are you trying to challenge prejudice, discrimination, oppressive practices?

  ❖ Are you trying to help the group members understand each other?

  ❖ Are you trying to stop some group members feeling oppressed and discriminated against?

◆ Do you respond immediately or deal with the matter later? What are the consequences of dealing with it immediately or waiting, or the consequences of dealing with it on an individual basis or in the whole group?

◆ Taking some action – doing something is usually better than doing nothing

◆ Reflecting and reviewing on the outcome of the actions you took and deciding on your next move.

As you talk through this you can use Handout 17. Give examples for each stage or you may find it helpful to use a worked example of a particular issue that is relevant to the group. Then ask participants to work in small groups to decide how to approach a specific situation. You can either use some of the examples that have come up already in this session or make up some other ones pertinent to the group. They need to be quite specific so that people can practice working out their answers.

Examples from the community space scenario could be:

◆ Someone objecting to the idea of women-only space on the grounds that it will lessen the flexibility of the space. (Issues about why women want safe space – Lesbian women and Muslim women have different reasons but both may need women-only space)

◆ Someone commenting that 'handicapped' people don't use facilities and so it's pointless putting in 'disabled' toilets. (issues of language – Disabled people and accessible toilets, and attitudes about the rights of Disabled people to use community facilities and understanding why Disabled people often don't because the basic facilities are lacking)

◆ Someone objecting to people with mental health problems being able to use the space and making comments about them being dangerous (Issues about how prevalent mental ill health is – one person in four will suffer some form of mental ill health, and that the term mental ill health can cover a wide range of diagnosis – from depression to paranoia, very few of which are dangerous to others. Most people lose confidence and need support to regain their sense of self esteem)

◆ Someone voicing concern about children using the centre because of the noise, the need to have storage space and that they should be at home with their mothers leaving the community space for older people who would appreciate it (Issues about the role of mothers, attitudes to children, need to enable children to feel part of a wider society).

Approaches to equality

There are a number of different approaches to equality that you may come across – here is a summary of four of them to show the range of reactions.

1 Promoting the assimilation of the minority community into the majority society/community

This is based on the idea that the group has little need to change to meet the needs of different communities. There are assumptions about:

◆ That the group is non-discriminatory

◆ That everyone has equal access to the group and its provision

◆ That the needs of all people are the same

◆ That minorities should adapt to and accept the current situation

◆ That the minority community are the problem.

The consequences are that the minorities are:

◆ Denied access to appropriate provision

◆ Expected to take what is on offer

◆ Excluded from decision-making

◆ Put in a situation where their needs are not considered.

2 Promoting the sharing of different cultures

This is based on the idea that if we all know a bit more about each others cultures there will be less discrimination and oppression. There are assumptions about:

◆ Greater knowledge will address the 'isms'

◆ That knowing more will lead to individual and organisational changes

◆ That the only needs of minorities relate to culture

◆ That there is a static culture which can be learnt by others

◆ That power imbalances between different groups and communities are not important.

The consequences are that:

◆ Discrimination and oppression continue unchallenged

◆ Culture dominates

◆ Oppressed people are exploited – being asked to share their experiences/culture/raise other awareness

◆ The minorities do not gain much from such exchanges.

3 Promoting equality of access, opportunities and outcomes

This is based on the idea that groups can challenge individual and institutional discrimination and oppression. There are assumptions about:

◆ Current practices may not meet the needs of minorities

◆ That different minorities have specific needs which should be addressed

◆ Positive action is important

◆ Majorities have a role in challenging discrimination and oppression of minorities.

The consequences are:

◆ That minorities have choice

◆ That minorities have greater confidence in the group

◆ That more resources are available to minorities

◆ That there is a greater dialogue between communities.

4 Promoting equal rights and justice

This is based on the idea that groups have a role to play in developing minority communities. The assumptions are that:

◆ Discrimination and oppression restrict the life choices of minorities

◆ That majority groups can collude with discrimination and oppression of minorities

◆ That groups need to change

◆ That minorities have a right to be involved and benefit from groups

◆ That many groups do not meet the needs of minorities.

The consequences are:

◆ That provision becomes more relevant to minorities

◆ That some separate and relevant provision is resourced and developed

◆ That groups become more accountable to all minorities in their community

◆ That the needs of minorities are appropriately met

◆ The group will have a greater awareness of minority presence.

An approach to tackling conflict

◆ Checking out what you have heard or seen

◆ Deciding what is behind the words or actions

   ❖ Is it based on misinformation (such as the numbers of people seeking asylum)?

   ❖ Is it the result of well-intentioned but ill-thought out behaviour (treating disabled people inappropriately – the 'does he take sugar' syndrome)?

   ❖ Is it designed to upset and offend (deliberate use of words or excluding behaviour such as turning their back on someone)?

◆ Deciding on the best approach

   ❖ Do you need to correct the information and present accurate facts and data?

   ❖ Do you need to explain why the behaviour is causing offence and distress? Do you need to stop the behaviour and deal with it later?

◆ What do you want to achieve?

   ❖ Are you trying to challenge, prejudice, discrimination, oppressive practices?

   ❖ Are you trying to help the group members understand each other?

   ❖ Are you trying to stop some group members feeling oppressed and discriminated against?

◆ Do you respond immediately or deal with the matter later? What are the consequences of dealing with it immediately or waiting, or the consequences of dealing with it on an individual basis or in the whole group?

◆ Taking some action – doing something is usually better than doing nothing

◆ Reflecting and reviewing on the outcome of the actions you took and deciding on your next move.

Reflective Journal

To be completed after each 4 hours of group work

Name of participant _____

Name of Tutor/s _____

1 Give a brief description of the topics covered by the group work and highlight your main areas of learning.

2 What did you think and feel about the group? What did you contribute to the group and its work?

3 Did you find anything difficult in the session and/or are there areas you would like us to cover again?

Portfolio question

You need to demonstrate an understanding of the issues of inclusion and exclusion within groups and networks.

For level 2 You should identify some of the processes which can lead to groups/networks becoming exclusive – use examples to illustrate your points. Then give two suggestions of how groups and networks can remain open and inclusive.

For level 3 You should analyse in some detail the issues around inclusion and exclusion that relate to groups and networks. Then you should explain how you could devise a strategy to ensure that a group remains inclusive and open. Give some examples of the main points within your strategy.

(Complete during the week)

Make notes of anything or thoughts that have occurred during the week which you feel challenged you, or re-emphasised your beliefs/experiences.

Tutor's comments

Signature of participant _____

Signature of tutor/s _____ Date _____

Roles within groups

Roles within groups
Session Plan 11 and 12

◆ **Target audience**

People involved in and working with community groups

◆ **Length of session**

2 x 2-hour sessions; four hours in total

◆ **Session aim(s)**

- To explore current and future roles people can take within groups and networks

◆ **Session outcomes**

At the end of the session students/trainees will...

- Demonstrate an awareness of the roles they take in groups and the impact they have on a group

◆ **Indicative content**

- Roles taken within groups

- Presenting yourself in a group

- Awareness of the impact you have on a group and its effectiveness

- Managing change.

Detailed Session Plan 11

Time	Content	Exercise/Method	Resources	Notes core topic or optional if time
0.00	Warm up			
0.10	Reflective journals; aims of session	Collect any journals. Tutor to explain aim of session	Session plan	
0.15	Roles participants take within groups – As worker/or member. Maintaining and supporting groups	Exercise to look at the roles people are taking in their groups – formally and informally	Tutor Prompt Sheet 35 Worksheet 11	
0.30	Understanding own approach to groups and team working	Group behaviour questionnaire; what can they bring to a group? What impact might they have?	Worksheet 12	
1.00	Deciding your role in groups	Case studies	Case study scenarios	
1.40	Presenting yourself within a group	Draw a picture of yourself explaining what you can offer to a group	Tutor Prompt Sheet 36	

Roles people take in groups

The aim of this session is to get people to bring together their learning from this course and to consider the roles they take in groups and why.

The roles that we take are determined by a mixture of:

◆ The situation
◆ The way we work in groups
◆ What role we are ascribed
◆ What roles we decide to take
◆ Our skills and expertise
◆ Other members of the group.

Amongst other factors.

Worksheet 11 is an individual exercise to get people to think about their formal and informal role in one group. When they have done this they can share with another person who knows a bit about them.

Worksheet 12 is another individual exercise to help people think through the more personal aspects of working in a group.

Exercise on roles in groups

Using the information gained from this course, fill in this sheet on your own and then share it with one other person who knows something about you and/or your group by now.

Briefly describe one group that you are involved in	
Describe your formal role in this group	
Describe any informal roles you take in this group	
Describe how others in the group see you and your role	
Why do you think you ended up in these roles?	

My Group Behaviour

The following are a series of questions about your behaviour as a member of a group. Answer each question as honestly as you can. Remember, there are no right or wrong answers, the questions are to help you assess your behaviour, and identify areas in which you may want to change or develop.

1 *I offer facts, provide information and make suggestions that are relevant to the task of the group.*

Rarely ☐   Often ☐

2 *I take a lead in initiating activities that contribute to the group.*

Rarely ☐   Often ☐

3 *I share relevant resources, such as books, films, leaflets, tape-slides and contacts.*

Rarely ☐   Often ☐

4 *I notice when the discussion is moving away from the point and attempt to bring it back*

Rarely ☐   Often ☐

5 *When the direction of the group is unclear I try to summarise where I think we have got to, to enable us to be clearer about future developments.*

Rarely ☐   Often ☐

6 *I try to be honest about my feelings and responses.*

Rarely ☐   Often ☐

7 *Before contributing to the discussion I think about whether what I want to say will help the group achieve its task, or whether I am saying it to score a point.*

Rarely ☐   Often ☐

8 *I try to support participants who are finding it difficult to contribute to the group, or to make themselves understood.*

Rarely ☐   Often ☐

9 *I think about and take into consideration, how cultural and life experiences may be affecting the behaviour of individuals in a group.*

Rarely ☐   Often ☐

10 *I try to build others' self-esteem by appreciating their abilities, strengths, talents and contributions.*

Rarely ☐   Often ☐

11 *I take responsibility for my own learning and to some extent for how successful the group is.*

Rarely ☐   Often ☐

12 *I notice group members who are being destructive or difficult and try to find strategies for coping with them.*

Rarely ☐   Often ☐

What impact do you think you have on groups that you are part of?

Group Work Skills • **Session Eleven**
Federation for Community Development Learning

Deciding your role in a group

There are seven case study scenarios based on situations that community development workers might find themselves in. Some are more complex than others. These case studies can be substituted by those you have developed or which may be more relevant to your learners.

Ask people to work in groups of two or three and discuss what an appropriate role might be and why?

Ask them to be prepared to feedback to the whole group and allow time for discussion.

You are supporting a tenants and residents association on an estate on the edge of town. It is quite a small group with an active chair person, a membership secretary who is always willing to take on tasks although he works full-time and a couple of other women with families and limited time. The group has been negotiating with the council over getting the estate improved and repairs made to their homes. It is coming up to election time for the local council elections. The town used to be solid Labour but over the past few years the Liberal Democrats have gradually been increasing their number of councillors and they are beginning to threaten the Labour Party's overall control of the council.

Case Study 1

The chair person comes to you and says that she had been getting on well with the officers and councillors looking to put together a bid for the estate regeneration. At the last meeting they said that this would all be jeopardised unless the tenants group got rid of the membership secretary as he is well known as a Liberal Democrat. They have heard that he is standing in the ward for election to the council. The bid has to be made within the next couple of weeks, before the outcome of the election is known.

What would you consider to be your role in this situation?

You work as a community safety worker, trying to get local people (individually and through groups) to look at issues of safety as it affects them in their local area. You are approached by a member of the committee which runs activities for older people at the Housing Association complex. They tell you that they have seen some travellers parking up on the car park outside the recently vacated garden centre and they want you to get rid of them. They argue that the travellers will lead to an increase in robberies, they will create a mess which will become a health hazard, and they will mug older people. They have contacted the local pub and some shops and asked them to ban them from their premises.

Case Study 2

What would you consider your role to be in this situation?

You work in a local family centre in an inner city area, running groups on parenting skills, enabling contact between parents and children, etc. Most of the people who use the centre have been referred by the local Social Services department. You are approached by a number of parents who say they suspect some local people of being paedophiles. They want to use the copier at the centre to make some posters outing these people and organising a demonstration to make them leave the estate.

Case Study 3

You have been working within the centre's policy of trying to empower the people who use it. You are aware of the background of these parents and through your multi-agency work have some knowledge about people with criminal convictions for sex offences that live on the estate.

What would you consider your role to be in this situation?

A group of Disabled people started a campaigning organisation to improve the situation for Disabled people in their area. They then gained some lottery funding to provide an advice and advocacy service to Disabled people. The funding is coming to an end and the group approach the council to try and get some money to keep going. The response is that the only money available is for any group that is willing to run a carers support service, as the council has recognised that there are few services for carers. The council argues that its own advisors can take over the advisory service although you know that it works on a medical model and is not committed to the empowerment of Disabled people.

Case Study 4

What would you consider your role to be in this situation?

A housing association based in an inner city area is developing a small complex of houses and bungalows. In the complex there is a community room, which the older people in the complex have annexed as their own. As more families move

into the houses so the demand for some kind of youth facilities increases. Some of the young people approach the housing association and ask if they can have access to the community room and put in some equipment that they could get grants for. You approach the older people who are vehement that they do not want to share their space. They say there is no room for equipment, that the place is fully used, that they don't want the noise, and so on.

What do you consider your role should be in this situation?

You are working with a small environmental group, originally advising them on the development of a millennium green for their area. Since then you have been involved in supporting their different activities which have been held on the

green and to raise awareness of local environmental matters. They decide that they want to become a charity so they can apply for more funding to develop their group and the scope of its activities. They need more people to join the committee to raise the numbers to a level considered acceptable by the charity commissioners.

They ask you to become a committee member and therefore a charitable trustee for their organisation. You are employed by a local PCT with a wide ranging health remit.

What would you consider your role to be with this group? Will you accept their offer?

You work for a building society and as part of their commitment to supporting local good causes you ended up becoming involved in a small local history project which aims to involve young people in knowing more about their area.

You recommended this group as a beneficiary of the money raised by savers of the building society. As a result of this they received some money to develop their project. They now want to apply to the Heritage Lottery for some other funds to be able to make a video of the area and some of its famous landmarks. They ask if you will take on the role of treasurer.

What do you consider your role should be in this situation? Will you take up their offer?

Detailed Session Plan 12

Time	Content	Exercise/Method	Resources	Notes *core topic or optional if time*
0.00	Warm up			
0.10	Making changes to your role; moving within and out of a group	Making an action plan for your next steps	Tutor Prompt Sheet 38 Worksheet 13	
0.30	Where to get support to move forward?	Group discussion/resource balloons	Tutor Prompt Sheet 39 Resource balloons – several for each person	
1.00	Evaluation	Group based evaluation	Any visual version would be suitable	
1.30	Portfolios and arrangements for handing in	Tutor input		Any more OCN forms
1.40	Final game and goodbyes			
2.00	End			

Moving on

This exercise is designed to help people think through the roles they are in now and what changes they need to make. Talk about the importance of changing our roles to meet the needs of groups; and also to build on our strengths and to develop our own personal and professional skills.

This four-step action-planning approach can be used in many different settings and situations. Here it is being used to help people think about changing their roles and what might help or hinder them.

They may choose to complete this on their own, with others from the same group or with people they have grown to trust on the course.

Worksheet
13

Four steps for action planning

Step ❶ Clarifying

Take a short time to note down features of your present situation and roles you are in which you wish to change. Try to make a statement about what you would rather have instead – your desired outcome.

Step ❷ Analysing

Think about the driving and restraining forces in your present situation, things that move you and your group forward or hold you back. These include the needs, drives, aspirations, fears and feelings of other people as well as yourself.

Reducing or removing the restraining forces can most readily achieve movement in the right direction. If driving forces are increased first, the result is likely to be an increase in restraining forces.

Try asking:

◆ Do I have a clear statement about where I wish to be?

◆ Have I identified all the important variables?

◆ Do I have reasonably accurate information about the strength of the various forces?

◆ What additional information do I need and how can I get it?

◆ How do the forces inter-relate?

Use the action plan sheet to show your driving and restraining forces.

Step ❸ Follow Up

Follow up the action plan by asking the following questions:

◆ What is the relative importance of the forces I have identified?

◆ To which people and forces do I have access – what is my point of entry?

◆ Where do I have influence for change?

◆ Where and for what reason might there be readiness to change?

◆ What are the linkages between people that are now or might be important for changes?

◆ What happens if I fail to attempt to make changes?

Step ❹ Action Plan

Use the action plan sheet to try to itemise the individual steps you need to make towards your desired state.

Group Work Skills • **Session Twelve**
Federation for Community Development Learning

My Action Plan

Desired outcome	
Driving forces	
Restraining forces	
Possible change to either forces, such as hindrances to minimise, alliances to encourage	
Action and target date	
Who will help?	

Getting support to move on

Once everyone has decided what their next steps might be, they may need advice and guidance as to where to get appropriate support and information.

Give out the resource balloons, people can have as many as they want. Around the edge of each balloon they write a question… 'where can I get xxxx?' They then pin their balloons onto a wall space which everyone can reach. People then look at everyone else's balloons and if they know an answer they write it into the balloon.

You need to check if some of them are left blank and see if you can encourage answers. You may need to check the accuracy of some of the replies.

People can either collect their own balloons with the answers or you could get them all typed up as a resource list and sent out to everyone.

A Resource Balloon

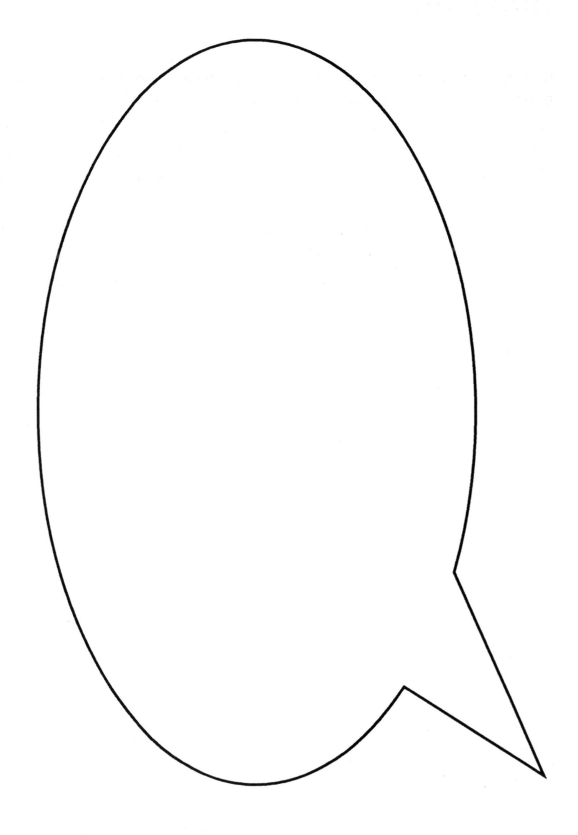

Reflective Journal

To be completed after each 4 hours of group work

Name of participant _____

Name of Tutor/s _____

1 Give a brief description of the topics covered by the group work and highlight your main areas of learning.

2 What did you think and feel about the group? What did you contribute to the group and its work?

3 Did you find anything difficult in the session and/or are there areas you would like us to cover again?

Portfolio question

You need to demonstrate an understanding of the roles that you take in groups and the impact you have on a group.

For level 2 You should explain the key roles you take in groups, with examples, and describe the interpersonal skills you need to work effectively in a group.

For level 3 You should describe your role with groups and analyse the factors that have led to this position. Describe the interpersonal skills required for effective group work over a period of time and suggest ways that these can be developed within a group.

(Complete during the week)

Make notes of anything or thoughts that have occurred during the week which you feel challenged you, or re-emphasised your beliefs/experiences.

Tutor's comments

Signature of participant _____

Signature of tutor/s _____ Date _____